# CALIGULA

Sam Wilkinson provides an accessible introduction to the reign of Caligula, one of the most controversial of all the Roman emperors. Caligula's policies have often been interpreted to be those of a depraved tyrant. This study provides a reassessment of this controversial reign by scrutinising the ancient literary sources that are so hostile to Caligula, and by examining the reasoning behind the policies he enforced. Key topics discussed include:

* Caligula's early life and accession to power
* Caligula's relationship with the senate
* How far Caligula's domestic and foreign policies can be judged to be a success
* Why Caligula was assassinated in AD 41, only four years after his accession to power.

With a guide to primary and secondary sources, a chronology and a detailed glossary, *Caligula* is an invaluable study of the reign of this fascinating Emperor.

**Sam Wilkinson** is a historian attached to the Classics Department of Royal Holloway, University of London. His research centres around the Julio-Claudian emperors.

# LANCASTER PAMPHLETS IN ANCIENT HISTORY

GENERAL EDITORS: ERIC J. EVANS AND P.D. KING

Hans Pohlsander, *Emperor Constantine*
David Shotter, *Augustus Caesar*
David Shotter, *The Fall of the Roman Republic*
David Shotter, *Nero*
David Shotter, *Roman Britain*
David Shotter, *Tiberius Caesar*
Richard Stoneman, *Alexander the Great*
John Thorley, *Athenian Democracy*
Sam Wilkinson, *Caligula*

# CALIGULA

Sam Wilkinson

Routledge
Taylor & Francis Group

LONDON AND NEW YORK

First published 2005
by Routledge
2 Park Square, Milton Park, Abingdon, Oxon OX14 4RN

Simultaneously published in the USA and Canada
by Routledge
270 Madison Avenue, New York, NY 10016

*Routledge is an imprint of the Taylor & Francis Group*

© 2005 Sam Wilkinson

Typeset in Garamond and Scala by RefineCatch Limited, Bungay, Suffolk
Printed and bound in Great Britain by TJ International Ltd, Padstow, Cornwall

All rights reserved. No part of this book may be reprinted or
reproduced or utilised in any form or by any electronic,
mechanical, or other means, now known or hereafter
invented, including photocopying and recording, or in any
information storage or retrieval system, without permission in
writing from the publishers.

*British Library Cataloguing in Publication Data*
A catalogue record for this book is available from the British Library

*Library of Congress Cataloging in Publication Data*
Wilkinson, Sam.
    Caligula / Sam Wilkinson.
        p. cm. – (Lancaster pamphlets in ancient history)
    Includes bibliographical references and index.
        1. Caligula, Emperor of Rome, 12–41.   2. Rome–History–Caligula, 34–41.
    3. Emperors–Rome–Biography.   I. Title.   II. Series.
    DG283.W55 2005
    937′.07′092–dc22
    [B]                        2004012850

ISBN 0–415–35768–3 (hbk)
ISBN 0–415–34121–3 (pbk)

# CONTENTS

# ILLUSTRATIONS

# ACKNOWLEDGEMENTS

I am grateful to David Shotter, who not only gave me invaluable advice in the production of this work but also kindly allowed me to use both his glossary of Latin terms from the previous pamphlets, and Figures 1 and 3.

# ABBREVIATIONS

All abbreviations are taken from Liddell, Scott and Jones's *Greek Lexicon* (9th edn, Oxford 1940) and Lewis and Short's *Latin Dictionary* (Oxford 1879) where possible. All editions are Loeb Classical Library (London, Heinemann).

| | |
|---|---|
| D.C. | Cassius Dio, *Roman History* (London, 1914–27) |
| *I.L.S.* | *Inscriptiones Latinae Selectae,* ed. H. Dessau, 3 vols. (Berlin, 1892–1916): vol. 2 (1902) |
| Ph. *In Flacc.* | Philo Judaeus, *In Flaccum* (London, 1941) |
| Ph. *Leg.* | Philo Judaeus, *Legatio ad Gaium* (London, 1962) |
| Pliny *H.N.* | Plinius the Elder, *Naturalis Historia* (London, 1938–62) |
| J. *A.J.* | Flavius Josephus, *Antiquitates Judaicae* (London, 1965) |
| J. *B.J.* | Flavius Josephus, *Bellum Judaicum* (London, 1927) |
| Sen. *Brev. Vit* | Seneca, *De Brevitate Vitae*, Moral Essays (London, 1928–35) |
| Sen. *Ira* | Seneca, *De Ira*, Moral Essays (London, 1928–35) |
| Suet. *Calig.* | Suetonius, *De Vita Caesarum* (London, 1913; reprinted and revised 1998) |
| Suet. *Galb.* | Suetonius, *De Vita Caesarum* (London, 1914) |
| Tac. *Agr.* | Tacitus, *Agricola*, Dialogus (London, 1914) |
| Tac. *Ann.* | Tacitus, Annales, *Histories and Annals* (London, 1925–37) |
| Tac. *Hist.* | Tacitus, Historiae, *Histories and Annals* (London, 1925–37) |

# 1

# INTRODUCTION

The Emperor Gaius, otherwise known by his nickname Caligula ('little boot'), came to power at the age of 24 in March AD 37, only the second man to inherit the principate. By January AD 41 he had been assassinated. For someone whose reign was so short he has certainly achieved notoriety. The name Caligula is synonymous with vice, depravity and even insanity. He was the standard example of the archetypal tyrant to his literary contemporary Lucius Annaeus Seneca. And that is how posterity has remembered him. But is there really historical evidence to support such a tradition? This work intends a reappraisal of Gaius by not only investigating his policy at home and abroad in the four years of his reign but also by comparing and contrasting this with those of his immediate predecessors and successors. His reign is too short to be treated in isolation. Only by searching for consistency of government with regard to Roman policy at the time can his reign be fully evaluated. Did Gaius diverge from Augustan precedent? Did he innovate in his domestic government or foreign policy, and if so were such actions successful? Did his successors continue his work? By studying Gaius in this wider context, and by concentrating on his government, taking a more rigorously political approach, light will be shed on the value and consequence of his reign.

It is essential to investigate Gaius' government, and his relations with the various strata of Roman society, in order to understand how his assassination came about after only four years. In other words, who was against Gaius and why?

The principate that Caligula inherited was by no means an old institution. Augustus had spent years perverting the old Republic into a new Empire with a hereditary succession, and it was his sheer reputation and power, his *auctoritas*, that allowed him to put into practice his new ideas. There were always opponents of such an empire, adherents to the old 'republican' means of government, but Augustus' process of change was both slow and subtle, ending in Tiberius' accession. Tiberius had respected the old order of things, even if his manner did not always make this obvious; he had been a senator and so had friends in the senate on his accession. The 'republicans' could have seen hope in their new emperor – the first to inherit the position in Roman history. Tiberius' early government would certainly have appeased such men. However, Tiberius eventually withdrew to Capreae where he stayed from AD 26 until his death. This facilitated the start of a reign of terror headed by Lucius Aelius Sejanus. The interface between the senate and their emperor broke down with Tiberius' absence from Rome; a petrified senate merely rubber-stamped imperial 'orders' that originated from the island of Capreae. This in turn aided Sejanus in bringing court cases against his enemies. There were many victims, including Caligula's mother, Agrippina, and brothers, Nero and Drusus.

Eventually Tiberius acted against Sejanus' rising power and had him executed, which led to a further bloodbath as the city of Rome was purged of his supporters by an emperor paranoid about his own safety. Convictions filled Tiberius' last years, and even some of his friends fell, like Cocceius Nerva. By his death in AD 37 Rome had seen their *princeps* become more autocratic with every year; this was not Tiberius' wish, but the outcome of the political system, exacerbated by his retirement to Capreae and the paranoia surrounding the *maiestas* (treason) trials. Much blood had been spilled, and Tiberius' reputation was poor; he was hated by the senatorial class both for the deaths of their peers and for turning their body into a collection of people who merely ratified imperial orders, and by the people for the lack of games and shows provided by his reign. Tiberius had even banished actors altogether. He had, however, managed to maintain the line of succession and Caligula (with the young Gemellus) was to be his heir. Tiberius' rule had been austere and he respected the policies of his predecessor; there was no major attempt at expanding the Roman Empire, and no real innovations in his internal government.

When Caligula came to power his accession was celebrated across the Roman world. The *maiestas* trials had been put to an end and Rome looked forward to a new start under this new young emperor; on the shoulders of this son of Germanicus rested the hope of many.

# 2

---

# UPBRINGING AND ACCESSION

Caligula was born on 31 August AD 12 at Antium (Suet. *Calig.* 8) to a distinguished family. Through his mother Agrippina the Elder, daughter of Julia, he could trace a direct bloodline to Augustus himself and the powerful Julian family. His father's family were no less distinguished; Caligula was the great-grandson of Livia, the strong Claudian wife of Augustus. He was a true Julio-Claudian, born directly into the imperial family.

In AD 14 he accompanied his mother and father, the popular Germanicus, to the Rhine where they would remain until AD 17. Germanicus had inherited that title from Drusus who had crushed the Germans in 12–9 BC and reached the Elbe, and Caligula would be entitled to use it himself. Germanicus, sent there by Augustus, had instantly to deal with the death of the latter and the mutiny that followed on the Rhine. The accounts show that Germanicus certainly had trouble in putting it down. The soldiers saw the death of Augustus as a perfect time to complain about various conditions of service, and this got out of hand. Although the sources claim they offered Germanicus their services in obtaining the principate for himself, the following events make this unlikely. Regardless, Germanicus was loyal to the new emperor Tiberius. The tradition has it that Germanicus could not quell the rebellion, and that it was the sight of his wife Agrippina the Elder, with her retinue and son Caligula, leaving the camp to seek

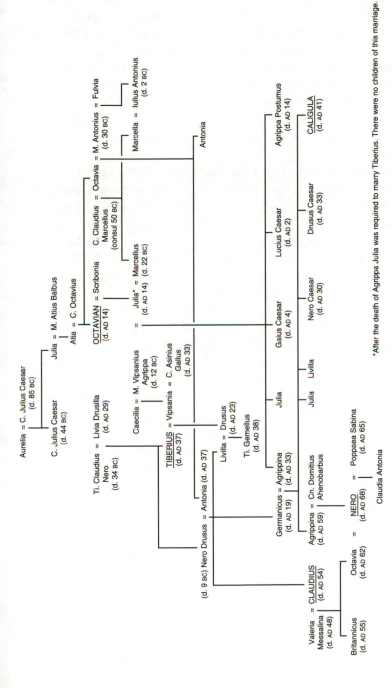

*Figure 1* Stemma of the Julio-Claudian family

solace with the tribe of the Treveri, that is supposed to have shamed the troops into subservience. Germanicus then let the men butcher the ringleaders of the mutiny and planned action in Germany to keep them busy. Whether Agrippina and Caligula were really involved in quietening the trouble is irrelevant; the anecdote shows the popularity of Caligula with the men. Moreover, Agrippina dressed Gaius in soldiers' boots (which is how he got his nickname) and even had him called Caesar Caligula when in camp. She clearly contrived to endear Gaius to the men.

Germanicus then crossed the Rhine in a punitive expedition in order to raise the morale of his troops. After a modest success, where he was able to reach the scene of the Varus defeat and raise a funeral mound to the dead, the Roman legions were almost ambushed by Arminius and had to retreat, which caused severe panic back at camp. Another anecdote has Agrippina stopping the bridge over the Rhine being destroyed by those worried by fear of losing the camp; this move made sure Germanicus and his men were not cut off and massacred. Tacitus would then have us believe she gave out clothes and shouted words of encouragement to the returning troops. Again, the reliability of the story is not too important; the sources play Caligula's mother up as a strong woman, level headed and loyal to her husband. The fact that she was actually with her husband on the Rhine backs this up. In AD 16 Germanicus attacked again, this time with a fleet. On its return a storm wrecked a large part of it; this would be his last action in Germany before Tiberius called him back to Rome for a triumph.

In AD 17 Germanicus enjoyed his huge triumph, and sitting in the chariot with him as he passed the adoring public was Caligula, almost 5 years old. This must have been one of his earliest, and most poignant, memories. Germanicus' exploits in Germany have not been seen as massive successes by modern scholars, but this did not affect his popularity with the Roman people and he secured for himself, and his children, a good reputation with the legions on the Rhine. However exaggerated the stories of Agrippina's role in the events are, she certainly contrived to make her son popular with the legions.

At 5 years old Gaius accompanied his parents on a new endeavour, this time to the East, where Germanicus was asked to settle the Armenian issue with Parthia. On the way they experienced huge displays of love from provincials as Caligula went on this grand tour. He even gave his first speech at Assos in AD 18 at 5 years old. Germanicus settled the dispute in Armenia by agreeing to the kingship of Zeno (Artaxias) and incorporated both Cappadocia and Commagene into the Empire. Germanicus died in AD 19 at 33 years of age amid rumours of foul play; this event set off a chain reaction that would see an obsessed Agrippina battle with Tiberius until it killed her. Germanicus' death at the height of his popularity, and amongst rumours that it was at the hands of Piso, who had been sent East by Tiberius, was key in establishing the legend and ensuring that his popularity would live on after him. The mini-biography of Germanicus at the beginning of Suetonius' *Life of Caligula* shows the extent of his popularity and renown.

In AD 20, at 7 years old, Caligula accompanied his mother and the ashes of his father back to Italy. Again, they were received everywhere by a huge crowd, this time in mourning. Neither Tiberius nor Livia attended the funeral. Germanicus' popularity across the Empire was huge; the rightful heir to the unpopular Tiberius had died and Agrippina was to do her utmost to make sure one of her sons would receive what she saw as Germanicus' by right. She had witnessed how a headstrong Livia had schemed and managed against all odds to procure the principate for her son Tiberius, and she seemed obsessed with doing the same.

From Germanicus' death onwards Rome seemed to become divided between the supporters of Agrippina, who used the popularity of Germanicus to her advantage, and the supporters of the praetorian prefect Sejanus. Tiberius and Agrippina openly quarrelled anyway, and this was exacerbated by Sejanus' attempts to remove Agrippina's family from the succession. This developed into treason trials and the convictions of Agrippina's friends as she continued to provoke the *princeps*. In AD 24 the names of Gaius' older brothers were included in the annual oath of allegiance for Tiberius, possibly at Agrippina's instigation. This would be entirely in keeping with her actions to ensure the popularity of Gaius with the Rhine legions and led to severe reproach from Tiberius and more convictions for her supporters.

In AD 27 Tiberius left for Capreae and a 15-year-old Caligula moved in with his great-grandmother Livia. There he met the three Thracian princes (Rhoemetalces, Polemo and Cotys) and Herod Agrippa, all of whom would remain his friends and benefit from his later rule. Two years later Livia passed away and Caligula gave the funeral oration. He then moved in with Antonia. Livia has often been seen as a large influence on her son Tiberius, and with her out of the picture it may have been easier for both Sejanus and for Tiberius himself to get their way. In AD 30 Caligula's brother Nero committed suicide; he could not hold his tongue about his views on the emperor, a trait he undoubtedly picked up from his mother. In the year AD 31 Caligula was made a priest and at the ceremony there was a show of popularity towards him from the populace. He was then called to Capreae as a man of 18; in the same year Sejanus finally fell, but this did not stop the death of Agrippina and Drusus two years later in AD 33.

Caligula had experienced first hand the power struggle between his mother and Sejanus; he was aware of his popularity, but had not spoken out to aid his family. As a result he had saved his own life; he had luckily been too young to threaten Sejanus during the lifetime of the latter. Gaius would stay on Capreae with Tiberius until his accession in AD 37. On that island he would have been privy to the ravings of Tiberius, and seen the continuation of the *maiestas* trials. In fact, for most of his life these would have been a common occurrence. He saw the reign of Tiberius descend into more bloodshed and become more autocratic as the emperor retired to Capreae. One man was even accused of plotting against the young Gaius. Having no doubt been convinced by his mother of his birthright to rule, and being acutely aware of his own popularity, it must have come as no major surprise when Tiberius named him joint heir with Gemellus in AD 35.

Caligula had, however, no experience of governing; the extent of his education in this respect was being made quaestor for AD 33. He had no formal training or major experience of the senate. He had been given no commands in the field, such as those given to Gaius and Lucius by Augustus. Instead he had been indoctrinated by an ambitious mother of the importance of his own family and their right to rule; he had been convinced of his own nobility; he had witnessed the autocracy of Tiberius' later years.

On 16 March AD 37 Tiberius died and Gaius acceded to the throne as a 24-year-old unknown; all he had was the popularity of his family and the reputation of Germanicus to introduce him to the Roman world. This family was very important to him, and would be honoured and used as a political tool throughout his reign.

The accession was a smooth one. Macro and his praetorian guard immediately swore allegiance to Gaius, and he sent word to the legions around the Empire to do the same. Two days later the senate followed suit; they were unlikely to go against the army, and they had no reason yet to dislike Gaius. Gaius accompanied the body of Tiberius from Misenum to Rome and did not arrive in the city until 28 March. The journey to the capital saw joyous crowds greeting the emperor and offering sacrifices to him; Caligula was used to such receptions by now. The people of Italy were ecstatic at the replacement of Tiberius.

Macro had the will of Tiberius declared null and void on the grounds of poor health; this way Gemellus had no formal position as joint heir, which Tiberius had bequeathed. It is possible Macro had friends in the senate who helped with this. He was certainly instrumental in the transition of power from Tiberius to Caligula. Despite the will being declared null and void, Caligula still honoured Tiberius' legacies. The senate then granted Caligula all the powers and titles of Augustus in one block; Caligula only refused the title *pater patriae*, which sharply contrasted with Tiberius' reluctance to accept the principate altogether. It is believed that the Lex de Imperio Vespasiani, which probably conferred total imperial power, had its origins here. In short, Caligula was the first emperor to be given all the powers that Augustus and Tiberius had collected piecemeal over the years in one block from the outset; he had a free hand to do what he deemed best for the state. The popularity of Gaius' family allowed him to slip into the role of *princeps* with ease. The whole Roman world celebrated the accession of this completely unknown 24-year-old man, who had no background in politics or government and no experience of warfare. But what would this son of Germanicus do with his 'absolute power' (Suet. *Calig.* 14)?

# 3

## DOMESTIC POLICY

To investigate the government of Gaius over Rome the measures he took, for example his taxes, must be looked at. It is unlikely that the sources would concoct edicts entirely, but we must be aware of the gross exaggerations that surround them; so when both Suetonius and Dio talk of Gaius' move to repeal the censorship laws with regard to certain individual writers we should take this as historical fact, if there is no evidence to the contrary. Although reports in the ancient sources cannot easily be separated from subsequent interpretations, we must be wary of those interpretations given in the sources, and the evaluative comments found therein, and these must be treated with circumspection. From Seneca and Philo, through Josephus and Suetonius, and ending with Dio, none of the literary sources had any reason to praise Gaius; they all, however, had an interest in his shortcomings (see Appendix 1).

So, to analyse his policy, its effectiveness, economic viability and popularity with the various strata of Roman society must be investigated fully. Whether it was in any way detrimental to that society, and whether Gaius drastically changed the policies of his predecessors, must be looked at. Where Gaius did bring in new laws, were such changes beneficial to Roman society, government and the economy, and were his innovations maintained by his successors?

# FINANCE

The background to evaluating Gaius' government is a financial one; the sources claim Gaius was a bankrupt (Suet. *Calig.* 37; D.C. 59.2.6). Given the huge treasury Gaius supposedly inherited (either 2,300 or 3,300 million sesterces; D.C. 59.2.6) this is quite a charge, and would signify massive economic incompetence; we must investigate this first, ignoring the subjective claims of the sources that Gaius was a spendthrift and concentrating on the concrete charge that he was a bankrupt. Gaius may have been extravagant, but as long as he could afford to be, and the state did not suffer, there is nothing inherently wrong with this.

The difficulty of evaluating the fiscal policies of the Julio-Claudians, due to the division between the private wealth of the emperor and his income as head of state, has been pointed out. The large inheritance was partly illusory as not only Tiberius' but also Livia's bequests had to be paid, and donatives had to be given to the soldiers and people.[1] Moreover, such a large inheritance would have taken a vast amount of saving on the part of Tiberius, and so we should treat with scepticism the figure of 3,300 million sesterces as given in Dio and now look at the charge of bankruptcy.

The biggest piece of evidence against bankruptcy is that the early reign of Gaius' successor, Claudius, shows distinct affluence: he gave massive donatives, including 15,000 sesterces to each praetorian alone; he returned the fines Gaius had charged dishonest road contractors and even cancelled Gaius' taxes. Furthermore, he undertook expensive military campaigns, namely against Britain and Germany. He clearly had no financial problems in AD 41.

Gaius was still coining in precious metals in January of AD 41, and Claudius continued; this is not the sign of an empty treasury. Gaius supposedly brought in new taxes in late AD 40 to compensate, and these are depicted as ubiquitous and unpopular. Surely, though, these would not have been implemented in time to replenish an empty treasury, even coupled with Gaius' auctions in Gaul.

It is possible the lavish games Gaius put on and his extravagant rule, together with 'populist' policies (such as the abolition of sales tax, the renewal of popular elections, the reduction of the amount that those on the corn dole paid for the upkeep of statues, which will all be discussed later), brought in their wake the obvious criticism from certain quarters (i.e. the men of standing; the senators). Dio, when talking of Gaius' *congiaria*, abolition of sales tax and restoration of popular elections, says these acts 'grieved the sensible, who stopped to reflect that if the offices should fall once more into the hands of the many, and the funds on hand should be exhausted and private sources of income fail, many disasters would result' (59.9.7). Similarly Josephus castigates his 'squandering money on pleasures that would benefit no one but himself' (*A.J.* 19.207). These are just the evaluative comments we should try to avoid using, but they perhaps do show senatorial criticism of Gaius' legitimate expenditure. The 'sensible' may have *feared* bankruptcy, but that does not mean it happened. As ever, the tradition of Gaius simply became exaggerated over the years so that in the end he became a bankrupt (i.e. in Suetonius and Dio). Although the contemporaries of Gaius claimed he murdered the rich for property, and he was 'playing with the resources of the Empire', they do not charge him with bankruptcy (Sen. *Brev. Vit.* 18.5).

Gaius' donatives to the citizens on 1 June and 19 July AD 37 of 300 sesterces, his donative of 1,000 sesterces to the praetorians, 500 to the city guard, 300 to the army and night watch were not inconsistent with those of other emperors at all. Gaius' reign saw the first coin to be minted showing an imperial speech to the army, and this probably marked one of his donatives. The soldiers even received less at the accession of Gaius than at that of Tiberius. Claudius' 15,000 sesterces to his praetorians was obviously a lot more extravagant than Gaius' gift to them. According to Suetonius, Nero also gave a 400 sesterces donative to the people and supplied certain senators with an annual salary of up to 500,000 sesterces each on his accession. In short, Tiberius, Claudius and Nero were more generous.

Gaius took less than his predecessors from those on the corn dole for the construction of statues. The abolition of sales tax early in Gaius' reign was an extension of Tiberius' policy. The latter had cut it to 0.5 per cent, a reduction obviously popular across the board – although he had to raise it again. However popular, were all these fiscal policies sound? We are told that by late AD 40 'new and unheard of taxes' (Suet. *Calig.* 40) were brought in. One suggestion is that Gaius realised he had been overgenerous with the sales tax remission and so brought more taxes in. This possibility would mean that the abolition of the tax was economically unsound; but is there really evidence for this?

We know that the 1 per cent sales tax was introduced by Augustus, and in AD 17 it was dropped to 0.5 per cent because of the incorporation of Cappadocia and the revenue therefore gained from the province. Frank has conjectured that the tax brought in roughly 20 million sesterces annually thereafter which was paid into the *aerarium militare*.[2] The *Res Gestae* 17 shows that from AD 6 Augustus put 170 million into the fund as a one-off payment, and had both the sales tax and inheritance tax of 5 per cent going into it. On the assumption that Frank's calculation of *c*. 75 million sesterces being paid out to soldiers every year on retirement is more or less accurate, then reducing the sales tax from 1 per cent (as Tiberius had put it up again) to zero was taking away an income of around 20 million sesterces a year from that fund. We do not know the state of that fund on Gaius' accession, and we do not know how much the 5 per cent inheritance tax would bring in annually either, so it is difficult to ascertain whether the tax cancellation was irresponsible or not. However, Suetonius tells us that when on the Rhine Gaius sacked many chief centurions and 'then, railing at the rest for their avarice, he reduced the rewards given on completion of full military service to 6,000 sesterces' (i.e. they lost half their pension as set at 12,000 sesterces by Augustus; D.C. 55.23). Whether we take the view that only those dismissed lost half their pension, or whether we see a different interpretation of the Latin to refer to all the centurions of the Rhine army, Gaius would have made a saving on retirement payouts here, although how big we cannot be sure. Claudius, however, saw fit to restore the sales tax.

As far as the sources of the new taxes are concerned, Suetonius and Dio together mention food, lawsuits (2.5 per cent of the sum concerned), the wages of porters (12.5 per cent), prostitutes, taverns, artisans and 'wage-earning slaves'. We are given the scale of the tax only on lawsuits and porters. Neither source gives us the taxes in any intelligible way; they both smack of exaggeration. Which slaves earning money were charged? Who are these 'porters' – what do they do? Is not 12.5 per cent on the daily wage of porters incredibly high? Is it really likely that there was a 'fixed and definite charge' on any food sold anywhere in the city of Rome? How would such a tax be monitored and collected? Dio's 'rooms set apart in the very palace, and the wives of the foremost men as well as the children of the most aristocratic families that he shut up in these rooms and subjected to outrage, using them as a means of milking everybody alike' are surely to be distrusted (59.28.9). Josephus merely tells us that the tax rate was doubled, although which tax he does not say. As the taxes are not explained in our two sources furthest from the period – Suetonius and Dio – it is possible that the tradition about new taxes rides on the back of that of bankruptcy and so has been highly exaggerated.

Claudius cancelled Gaius' taxes, and so evidence for their precise nature is hard to find: they only survived six months. It is unlikely they would have supplied a huge amount of revenue anyway. Typically, Gaius' contemporaries have made no mention of such taxes. However, if we scan the taxes ascribed to Gaius by Suetonius and Dio we see that the prostitute tax was kept by his successors. Similarly, there was precedent for such a tax in Athens, Egypt, Cos and Syracuse.

In short, Gaius dropped certain taxes and probably levied others in his short reign; obviously taxes levied would be unpopular. A healthy treasury was left and so Gaius' fiscal policy over the four years was sound. When one looks at individual financial decisions our job is obfuscated by hostile sources. However, Gaius seems a good enough financier. Moreover, he innovated. To avoid a crisis like that of AD 33 under Tiberius, which came about due to his predecessor's hoarding of coinage, Gaius coined liberally. He attempted to bring in a heavier *dupondius* to differentiate that coin from the *as*, although this new coin was phased out under Claudius. Here we have a practical attempt to sort out a problem, however small. Other than that Gaius left the main essentials of denominations untouched. Gaius was also probably responsible for moving the mint from Lyons to Rome. If so, this move meant that the quantity and type of coinage, as well as the quality, could be regulated by the emperor himself. This was kept up by later emperors as such a move made administrative sense. He also seems to have closed down local mints in Spain, restricting the minting of coins away from Rome.

All evidence suggests that Gaius both inherited (although probably not as much as 3,300 million sesterces) and left behind a perfectly healthy treasury adequate for Claudius' high expenditure. Therefore if Gaius was extravagant he was not a bankrupt: he could afford his policies. The tradition of bankruptcy has been used to explain and exaggerate Gaius' actions, not only in the case of new taxes – and we can assume there were some, but which ones and how heavy they were has become unintelligible and unprovable – but also in connection with Gaius' auctions in Gaul and to explain the treason (*maiestas*) trials, which we will discuss in Chapter 5. Auctions in Gaul were common throughout Roman history and are therefore not evidence for bankruptcy. We cannot for sure know the extent of the auctions, or how much money they raised, despite the exaggerated anecdotes in the sources. For example, Suetonius has Aponius Saturninus buying 13 gladiators at 9 million sesterces and would have us believe so many transports were used in the Gallic auctions that they left a bread shortage in Rome; a similar charge is levied on Gaius concerning his bridge at Baiae. Such exaggerations cannot be proved, and so shed no light on the extent of Gaius' auctions.

Another financial innovation was his forcing of centurions to change Tiberius' name in their wills to that of Gaius. This paved the way for inheritances left not to the emperor as an individual but to the *princeps* as an institution. This would later be made law under Antoninus Pius. Of course, for those who did not want to leave anything to Gaius, this would have proved unpopular.

In conclusion, Gaius' reign was economically sound as a whole, although it is difficult to assess individual financial policies owing to the limitations of the evidence and the exaggerations and hostility of the literary sources. However, even then it would seem Gaius abolished taxes where possible, and brought in new ones only if necessary. Furthermore, he even innovated in the area of finance, while doing his best to avoid a financial crisis. It is with this undermining of the 'bankruptcy' theory in mind that we must assess the rest of his domestic policy; it is noteworthy that Claudius' heavy spending received exactly the same criticism and was used to explain his 'murders'.

## FAMILY

Caligula certainly came to power with a clear idea of how he was to represent himself to the people of Rome. He immediately heaped honours on his direct family. He asked the senate to deify Tiberius, which proved unpopular and the subject was dropped. However, he would insist on certain privileges for his own family, and he showed no restraint in doing so. Although Dio would have us believe that Tiberius' funeral was a rushed affair, both Suetonius and the Arval Brethren records paint a different and more reliable picture; Tiberius was given a lavish send-off. Here Gaius supposedly drew more attention to his relationship with both Augustus and Germanicus than to the connection with his predecessor in the funeral speech. This would have been prudent considering the recent hatred for Tiberius. His parents' birthdays were celebrated with sacrifices by the Arval Brethren, and the *dies nefastus* which Tiberius had placed on Agrippina's birthday was removed. In a huge public display Caligula personally retrieved the ashes of Agrippina the Elder and Nero from Pontia and Pandateria, and returned them to Rome and the mausoleum of Augustus. No remains of Drusus could be found. September was renamed Germanicus (so it would naturally follow on from August) and two coins were issued, the obverse of one carrying the head of Agrippina and that of the other the head of Germanicus. Their birthdays were celebrated with games, and Gaius had a carriage bring the image of Agrippina into the arena; this was also commemorated on a coin. Seneca even has Gaius destroying the villa at Herculaneum where she had been held captive. A special *dupondius* coin was issued with both Nero and Drusus on, riding horses with their cloaks flowing behind them.

It was not only the dead who were to receive massive privileges: his grandmother Antonia was given the same honours that Livia had in her lifetime. She was named Augusta, given the privileges of the Vestal Virgins and made a priestess of Augustus. Unfortunately she passed away after only six weeks of Gaius' rule and so did not have time to enjoy her privileges. Naturally, the sources depict Gaius as driving her to death; in reality she was 73 years old, and Gaius clearly honoured this famous Roman. Claudius, the future emperor and brother of Germanicus, had been overlooked by Tiberius; he was now honoured with a consulship – the first for this 46-year-old. He was also to attend the games in the absence of Caligula.

The greatest and most innovative honours were to go to his sisters; they were also granted the right of the Vestals. At the games the sisters were allowed to sit with Gaius himself. They were to be included in vows, as Livia had been, and in the formula used by the consuls in the senate for forwarding motions. More importantly, they were included in the annual oath of allegiance to the emperor himself, which was hugely symbolic. A coin was issued with the heads of the three sisters Agrippina the Younger, Drusilla and Julia Livilla and the words *Securitas*, *Concordia* and *Fortuna*. There was no precedent for such a coin. After Drusilla's death in June AD 38, she was consecrated on 23 September, Augustus' birthday. Although novel, Barrett has shown it was not the huge break with Roman tradition that some have claimed; Tiberius blocked consecration for Livia, so it must have been an option.[3] The fact that the ceremony took place on the birthday of Augustus could only exaggerate her (and so Gaius') connections to the man.

In short, Gaius came to power with a clear policy to exploit his family ties. He exaggerated his links to Augustus and honoured his family as much as possible; he was using the popularity of both his mother, whom many saw as treated badly by Tiberius, and his father Germanicus. His coinage showed a distinct change to promoting the imperial house and his dynastic connections, particularly Germanicus and Augustus. To a certain extent, honour to the divine Augustus was a political necessity. Caligula made sure the dedication of the Temple of Augustus came about on his own birthday, 31 August AD 37, and put on massive games to celebrate; his sisters sat with him. A new coin was issued that showed Caligula sacrificing in front of the temple, and it was inscribed with *pietas* (piety or family duty). The connection with Augustus was again exaggerated by holding the celebration on his own birthday. Gaius' whole position as *princeps* was based on his family background, not on his *auctoritas*. By trying to elevate not only his deceased but also his living relations, he was exaggerating the importance of his family to a political end to show that both they, and so Caligula, were born to rule. Naturally he must have

cared for his sisters a great deal too, which explains their prominent position. The consecration of Drusilla was a master stroke: he
would then be the brother of a goddess; he was already the direct
great-grandson of a god.

While he played upon his link to Augustus, he played down his
connections to the unpopular Tiberius. Tiberius' name was left off
the urn for the ashes of Drusus, for example. This can be explained
further. Not only did Gaius want to separate himself from the last
emperor, who was clearly hated by many, but it was hard to base
his position as ruler on descent from Tiberius because Gemellus
was around. Gemellus was the true grandson of Tiberius, and had
been made joint heir with Caligula. Caligula therefore adopted
the boy and made him *princeps iuventutis*. This way he could outwardly be seen to embrace him into his family. The truth was very
different. In comparison to the honours the rest of Gaius' family
received Gemellus got very little. By adopting Gemellus, Gaius
put the boy into the next generation and therefore made him less
of a direct threat, while at the same time placating him. It was a
cynical move to keep him at close quarters before disposing of the
only legitimate threat to his own position and succession, as we
shall see later (p. 66).

So Caligula's policy of exploiting certain family ties to
strengthen his own position can clearly be seen; he wanted to
create an even stronger and more loved imperial house that was
related to gods themselves. Augustus and Tiberius had shown
decorum and restraint in honouring family members. Caligula, by
elevating his family so much, was reinforcing the hereditary
succession of the Empire to the exclusion of all capable men.

## ENTERTAINMENT

All the literary sources state that Gaius lavished gladiatorial
games and spectacles of every kind on his people. Dio states that
there was a performance every day; Suetonius talks of continual
stage plays; Philo attests Gaius' love of the games. He even went
so far as to allow people to go barefoot to the games, and to avoid
greeting him as this slowed down arrival at the shows. He also
allowed senators to bring hats and cushions with them. Gaius
increased the statutory number of gladiators allowed and recalled

the actors whom Tiberius had banished. In an attempt to improve the technicalities of the games he even reduced the amount of armour that the *murmillones* (a type of gladiator) wore and introduced both new boxers and the baiting of panthers.

Gaius obviously took a personal interest in the shows. He held yearly games for Agrippina and Drusilla; he celebrated Drusilla's birthday in AD 39 with two days of horse racing and did likewise for Tiberius' birthday. He extended the Saturnalia festival to five days as well. At the dedication of the temple of Augustus there were supposedly two days of races, a banquet for the senate, a feast for the people, and the games included the slaying of 400 bears and 400 lions. Individually the games and festivals were not that much more extravagant than the festivals or special occasions of the time: in AD 12 Germanicus had 400 animals slain – so Caligula had his family reputation to live up to. Claudius would follow suit, and in AD 41 had 600 beasts killed. It was the number of such grand games that was in direct contrast to Tiberius' austere regime; such festivities would obviously have been popular with the people of Rome (Josephus gives the reaction of the women, children and slaves in *A.J.* 19.130) and could be seen as Gaius' courting of popularity. He put on his own games to further this. However, he could afford such extravagances, as we have already seen. By all accounts Gaius turned Rome into a continual festival. As long as it was economically viable could anyone resent this? The answer, of course, is yes – the men of high standing, tradition and decorum – the senate.

Augustus had taken measures against performers when necessary; Tiberius had banished actors. Gaius recalled them, and not only indulged his passion for theatre and gladiatorial combat but seems to have had performers from the upper classes. Dio has Claudius forcing those equestrians who had performed under Gaius to do so one more time in order to shame them. Suetonius gives the story of senatorial charioteers and depicts this as an insult to the order; Claudius' shaming of equestrians suggests they had wanted to perform under Gaius; it is possible the senatorial charioteers did as well. Tiberius would not have let them, but Gaius indulged their passion. Tiberius had exiled men of standing who had done such a thing. Gaius was the first emperor to flout the rules preventing performances by such men.

Here there is a clear break in tradition, which could be seen as an insult to the orders.

Augustus had strictly regulated the seating at games, but Gaius supposedly scattered tickets to allow the *plebs* to take the equestrian seats. Augustus had aided people giving games; Tiberius had cancelled games in his own honour. Gaius revived the tradition, stopped by his predecessor, whereby two praetors were chosen by lot to put on games each year. This move, although popular with the masses that enjoyed the circus attractions, would have burdened the praetors. Claudius stopped this and dismissed games in his own honour. Similarly, Claudius did not ask for special games on his birthday six months into his reign; Gaius had held such games. Claudius was an emperor desperate to receive the blessing of the senate at the outset, and his measures *vis-à-vis* the spectacles go a certain way to proving the senators' dislike of Gaius' entertainments policy.

Claudius also put a ban on excessive repetition of games and tried to stop the equestrian games from going on for more than one day; this can be seen as evidence for abuse of the system under Gaius (i.e. games were spilling over from one day to the next). Similarly, by increasing the number of horse races and gladiators involved in everyday individual games Gaius was putting pressure on those holding games to spend more on them; it was, of course, the wealthy senators who would be putting on games.

The finances of the games were not a burden on the state. They were a problem for the individual, who felt compelled to live up to the standards set by Gaius for shows, even if these were not dramatically different from those for special occasions before him. Turning Rome into a festival was not showing enough decorum in the eyes of the traditionalists; Gaius even supposedly suspended mourning and all lawsuits so people could attend. Those forced to put on games would have felt the financial burden (and Gaius' restoration of elections in the *comitia* would mean candidates would have to spend money on canvassing; that is, by putting on shows and with bribery as under the Republic – see pp. 23–5). The obvious contrast to Tiberius' reign, and the taking of an ancient custom – that is, the man of *auctoritas* lavishing games upon the people – to a ridiculous extreme, was a perversion of tradition. Gaius' courting of popularity in this way turned Rome into a virtual circus. Senators standing for office who did not put on lavish spectacles would not be elected by the people. Gaius was gaining popularity at the expense of the senate, while the senators both financed the games and even performed in them as well.

The spectacles, although perfectly affordable by the state, and highly popular with the majority of Romans, were the trappings of a tyrant. Gaius' popularity would always be resented by the senate, especially if gained by such measures and not the traditional routes of politics or conquest. The senate was full of men who had achieved their *dignitas* through just such measures. Claudius reversed the policy as he knew the opposition which would accrue from the senate; Tiberius had had no desire for popularity with the people; the young Gaius went out of his way to achieve this.

## BUILDING WORKS

Gaius is regarded by Suetonius and Dio as a prolific builder, both at home and abroad. However, his reign was obviously too short for him to complete much of what he started or planned. He dedicated the temple of Augustus and the theatre of Pompey; Tiberius had not rushed them. For the service of the people we are told Gaius began an aqueduct near Tibur and an amphitheatre beside the Saepta. There must have been a need for more than the existing seven aqueducts so Gaius started two new ones – the aforementioned near Tibur, which would become the Aqua Claudia, and the Anio Novus.

He also seems to have started a harbour near Rhegium which Josephus regards as his only worthwhile building venture; Claudius reconstructed the harbour at Ostia in AD 42, so Gaius' Rhegium harbour has been seen in the light of trying to alleviate the continual grain supply problem that troubled Tiberius.[4]

Obviously the aqueducts, harbour, amphitheatre and dedications of both the temple of Augustus and theatre of Pompey would have been for the use and advantage of all the people of Rome. Tiberius had not had an extensive building programme at all and so Gaius returned to Augustan precedent. It is also possible that the Tullianum prison was extended under Gaius. Again, this would have had a practical purpose.

We also hear of Gaius' building works for his own pleasure. He had the palace extended, began a private racecourse – the Gaianum – which Claudius probably finished and used publicly, and supposedly had either one or two temples built to himself which we shall discuss on pp. 27–8. Pliny also refers to the luxurious houses of Gaius and Nero that surrounded the city in his time.

Gaius could clearly afford to build such features; the new aqueducts, amphitheatre and harbour were obviously beneficial, and in two cases practical public amenities that were continued. The building works also created jobs, fuelling the economy. The building of the new amphitheatre would perhaps have proved popular: football fans of today look forward to moving to a bigger ground. However, Claudius abandoned this plan. As for Gaius' personal building works, he was an emperor and behaved as one. We should be wary of exaggerations about, for example, the extensions made to the palace; Suetonius' claim that he built a bridge linking the Palatine to a new house on the Capitol is surely an error. Such a bridge would have had to be huge. Similarly, Dio's talk of Gaius setting up two temples to himself could well be false, as we shall see. Gaius was not the last emperor to build himself lavish apartments. We must also discount the generalisations in Suetonius that Gaius levelled mountains and built moles into the sea; without particulars we cannot judge.

## PUBLIC ADMINISTRATION

Gaius also made changes to governmental procedure, often showing a liberal and practical attitude. An early move was to publish the accounts of the Empire. Tiberius had suppressed his accounts and Gaius would be the last emperor to publish his. This is entirely consistent with the openness to the people that we see throughout his reign and raises the following question: if Gaius had been bankrupt would he really have published his accounts? As an act it is a perfectly sound one, taking its precedent from Augustus and showing honesty. That it was to fall by the wayside after him shows the increasingly absolute power of the *princeps*.

Another early measure was to revise the equestrian order. It had become 'reduced in numbers' (D.C. 59.9.5) under Tiberius and so

Gaius found the best men from the provinces and let them into the order. Tiberius had not revised the equestrian lists and so stopped such new men from entering the order; Gaius again innovated, with Julius Caesar and his advancing of Gauls as his precedent. He also let those equestrians who wanted to pursue a senatorial career wear the *latus clavus*, showing their intent.

Gaius broadened the equestrian order by bringing in provincials and gave the order a privilege; Claudius extended this policy by encouraging provincial senators. Gaius' move was the logical precursor of Claudius' act. It made sense to bring in and include in government the wealthiest provincials; it would not only supply the order with fresh blood but also promote Romanization and foster loyalty. Although in contrast to Tiberius' efforts to keep the orders closed to foreigners, Gaius' policy did continue. The first African equestrian can be found under Gaius.[5] Although such a move may have offended the traditionalists amongst the senate, it was a sound and progressive move that would encourage rich provincials to come to Rome, bringing their money with them. As Tiberius had let the number of the equestrian order drop, it was a sensible and pragmatic way to deal with that problem and would have no doubt been popular around the Empire.

Suetonius tells us that Gaius added a fifth 'level' of jurors to lighten their load and gave the magistrates unrestricted jurisdiction. This would speed up cases and mean that there would always be four levels of jurors available. (One level always had a year off.) Augustus had added a fourth level and so Gaius must have seen the need for another, perhaps due to an increase in law cases or prosecutions, especially after the *maiestas* trials under Tiberius and his absence from Rome. Gaius followed Augustan precedent, and his extra level of jurors remained intact. The unrestricted jurisdiction would put more power into the people's institutions, and so perhaps coheres well with the honesty and openness of his reign.

## ELECTIONS

One topic that has been a subject of much debate is that of the elections. Gaius transferred them from the senate to the *comitia*, but two years later had to return them to the senate. Suetonius (*Calig.* 16) sees this as an attempt to 'restore the suffrage to the people' as magistrates would now have to be voted in by the *comitia*, as in Republican Rome. Dio also sees this as a genuine attempt to re-establish a more broadly based government that failed because the candidates fixed things up between each other first so that only as many candidates stood as there were places available (59.20.4–5). He also claims the population had forgotten what it was like to transact governmental business as free men, and so they were lax in their duties.

A definite ramification of this would have been more canvassing by candidates and therefore more games. It indeed would be one reason for the frequency of games under Gaius, and why those standing for magistracies (on the whole senators) took so much offence at them. Hence the senate manipulated the number of candidates, possibly to avoid laying on games. This would have made elections meaningless. Tiberius' handing over of the voting to the senate was surely partly motivated by an attempt to stop such canvassing and the bribery associated with it. It also let the senators decide amongst themselves who would take up what posts, subject to the suggestions of the emperor himself, which in turn increased Tiberius' control. The senate were easier to manipulate than the whims of the people. All the candidates, if not senators, would be under senatorial patronage anyway. Under Tiberius the senate would probably have given their list, concocted with the emperor, to the *comitia* for formal ratification. The role of the *comitia* was purely ceremonial. An immense amount of money would be saved, as well as fuss with canvassing and bribery, as is typical of Tiberius' reign. But by doing so, Tiberius destroyed the electoral process entirely, even if it had become a sham, and turned an unelected body – the senate – into a nominating committee. Under Augustus the people had some involvement via free elections, but not under Tiberius. Perhaps Gaius' reversion to the Augustan system shows his appreciation of it, and is indicative of his desire to maintain popularity with his people at the expense of the senate.

Gaius, it would seem, genuinely attempted to restore the rights of the *comitia*, subject to his recommendations of course. This move, although in theory it should have been a popular one with the people, had to be rescinded. The people were probably apathetic in voting magistrates already vetted by Gaius, and even more so as there were often only enough candidates to fill the places, which varied in number annually. As Tiberius had stopped elections in the *comitia* after the death of Augustus in AD 14, Gaius' attempt to restore their privilege over twenty-three years later could simply have been too late to work. The original mechanism for summoning the electoral *comitia* may have been dismantled years previously as by now it was simply ratifying the choice of the senate and was probably more ceremonial than anything else. Much of the population would not have experienced such an election, and in a contented society politics is often dealt with apathetically by the working population.

The move, in keeping with Gaius' attempts to involve the people more and have a certain liberal feel to his reign, would have angered only one section of society: the senate. We must commend Gaius' attempt to return elections to the people as a policy, but we should note that in doing so he forced senators to spend their own money on canvassing and perhaps borrow to do so, just as Julius Caesar, when aedile, had borrowed from Crassus. Even if the senate did not set out to derail Gaius' attempts at elections in the *comitia*, Gaius saw the elections were not working and returned them to the senate. Gaius was perfectly prepared to cancel policy if it proved unworkable. The elections remained in the senate, although by Nero's reign it was common for the emperor simply to choose even the consuls.

## SENATE

Gaius enforced the individual taking of the oath by senators at the start of a New Year. This minor piece of ceremonial could be construed as a way of reminding the senators who was boss; all it could have done was annoy them. Gaius abolished the custom 'whereby some of the ex-consuls vote first or second according to the pleasure of those who put the question, and established the principle that such persons like the rest should cast their votes in the order in which they held office' (D.C. 59.8.6). Gaius seems to have been trying to impose a clearly defined fixed order of procedure, as seen under the Republic. Why Gaius would have wanted to meddle in the way the senate conducted business is obscure; we do have an unlikely personal reason in Dio – that it was to stop Marcus Silanus, his father-in-law, from voting first. Whatever the real reason, changing the senatorial voting system was probably not at the request of the senate here. Therefore, this would have simply angered the senate, showing them that Gaius could intervene at will. He seems to have gone out of his way to frustrate the institution, which shows he had a clear idea of how to rule the Empire, with the senate becoming less and less relevant.

## SOCIAL MEASURES

Gaius introduced a number of social measures as well, and he allowed the works of pro-Republicans, such as Cremutius Cordus, Titus Labienus and Cassius Severus to be reprinted (Suet. *Calig.* 16). This is in keeping with his liberal, progressive government that contrasted dramatically with Tiberius' reign. Similarly, the recall of exiles, freeing of prisoners and dismissal of untried charges wiped the slate clean for the Roman people on his accession. Tiberius had closed down the guilds, which had performed social functions, owing to their possible political activity; Gaius re-opened them. Claudius later closed them down again. Here we see part of Gaius' attempts to move away from the clandestine dealings of Tiberius' government from Capreae to a more open government, with Gaius in the centre of it. That many of these liberal acts (publishing of accounts, re-opening of guilds, restoration of elections, etc.) were not continued after Gaius does not make them unsound. On the contrary, their loss gave the emperor more power and the people less knowledge of the regime, and so less freedom. Gaius had a vision for a new Rome, and was not simply attempting to curry favour with his people. Furthermore, as governmental policies they were perfectly sound and would have been popular.

Gaius also accepted New Year's gifts, an old tradition that may have extended the interface between people and emperor. There was Augustan precedent for such a move. Naturally the sources have Gaius rolling about on his money and bringing in such measures because he was a bankrupt! Such anecdotes can be dismissed.

## RELIGION

Gaius' religious policy has been much discussed, especially his supposed belief in his own divinity. His personal religious beliefs are irrelevant to this work, unless they come out in his policy; it is his policy that must be investigated. As Pontifex Maximus he did not neglect his duties; he reorganised the college of the Salii and revived the custom of Nemi by finding a runaway slave to usurp the elderly priest. He also banned the priest of Jupiter from taking the oath in the senate house. His replacing of the priest of Nemi shows his interest in maintaining such institutions, as does his reorganization of the Salii. His attention to the precise nature of the oath for the *Flamen Dialis*, a minor religious post, shows his upkeep of tradition in the workings of religion. Although all minor religious technical points, they prove that religious organisations and traditions were positively maintained under Gaius. Gaius' policy on family deification is also an important one: he asked the senate to deify Tiberius as we have seen. Gaius similarly pushed for the deification of his sister Drusilla after her death, and this time with success. The only evidence we have for a cult being set up to her is in Dio, and so we should certainly treat this with circumspection as there is nothing contemporary to back up his story. Beyond this, Gaius' desire to be seen as a god has been much discussed. On this subject the Jewish sources – Philo and Josephus – should be left to one side for obvious reasons, and we must see if Gaius actively encouraged this in Rome. Only Suetonius and Dio talk of Gaius actually setting up a temple to himself in Rome.[6] The fact that Seneca, Philo and Josephus are quiet on this front is massively important; the latter two sources would have embraced clear evidence that Gaius believed himself to be a god. Suetonius does not even mention a cult for Gaius, and he had no reason to moderate his account, but he does mention a temple 'to his own godhead' (*Calig.* 22). Only Dio claims Gaius set up a cult to himself. It is illuminating to note that there is absolutely no numismatic or inscriptional evidence to back up the claim that there was an official cult set up to Gaius.

It is impossible to ascertain under what guise the emperor was officially worshipped as a god – if indeed he was. Dio says the senate decreed two temples to Gaius, but as this is not corroborated by any earlier sources it is prudent to discount the story. If there-fore one temple was set up to Gaius, by confirmation of the senate, and this was to his *numen* in association with Rome, then Gaius was actively following Augustan precedent. In AD 9 Augustus approved an altar on the Palatine to his *numen*. The talk of a cult to Gaius personally in Rome, as it is found only in the source furthest away from Gaius in time, must be doubted. Therefore Gaius was simply taking Augustan practice one step further in Rome by going from an altar to a temple. However, in popular conception, in certain parts of the Empire, the ruling emperor was equated with the gods anyway and Gaius, by wanting the deifica-tion of both Tiberius and then later Drusilla, seems to be promot-ing his connection to the gods. Nero later deified Poppaea; Gaius was not the last to deify a woman.

This connection to the heavens that Gaius seems to be encouraging ties in with his honouring of his family in general. In short, the more honours he could heap on his family, and the more gods or goddesses he was related to, the stronger his case for ruling would be. Gaius had no *auctoritas* on his accession, unlike both his predecessors, and this also explains his number of consul-ships: he had to prove himself in government. Similarly, his honouring of his family gave him more *auctoritas* indirectly.

## DISCUSSION

Throughout Gaius' policy we see measures that would inevitably court popularity: the games, the abolition of sales tax, the recall of exiles and actors – and not only with the people of Rome. He accentuated his ties with the army by his minting of a special coin that depicted his speech to the cohorts. Gaius erected new build-ings and turned Rome into a carnival. He even gave out food at stage plays.

Similarly, Gaius' attempts to return to a more liberal age – that is, with the cancellation of censorship on the Republican writings, the re-establishment of elections by the people, the freeing of prisoners and progressive moves such as the inclusion of foreigners in the equestrian order – could be seen as 'populist'. Gaius attempted to involve the people, or at least show them what was going on. He published accounts, and, even after the *maiestas* trials came back, he published not only the terms of the crime but also lists of those charged *in camera*. One of the few bad acts of domestic policy is given to us in Suetonius. He states that Gaius actually banned the erection of any statue to any living man anywhere without his permission. Such an edict is unlikely, and would surely be virtually impossible to police. In the context Suetonius gives it, it smacks of exaggeration: Gaius himself had just supposedly demolished the statues of famous men in the Campus Martius – we are not told how – to the extent that they could not be set up again with their relevant inscriptions. Then Gaius enacted his decree and went on to all but remove the writings and busts of Vergil and Titus Livius from all the libraries. This latter claim does not tie in with Gaius' republication of Republican writings and the liberal air of his reign; neither does his supposed smashing of statues. In such a context we should severely doubt such a decree ever existed; the silence of the other literary sources backs this up.

An overt part of Gaius' government was his obvious interest in being involved. He was granted 'full and absolute power' (Suet. *Calig.* 14; see also D.C. 59.3.2) and took all titles except *Pater Patriae* on his accession; in contrast to Tiberius he accepted all these without hesitation. It has been suggested that the original prototype of the 'lex de imperio Vespasiani' could date from this period.[7] If the *lex* did originate from the beginning of Gaius' reign then this preceded his governing and use of extreme power; that is, he used the 'full and absolute' power given to him. Gaius certainly was not scared to change the status quo domestically and remove power from the senate. In short, regardless of the date of the *lex*, Gaius used his power as emperor to the full.

Gaius immediately broke with tradition by holding four consulships in his four-year reign. This is a massive deviation from Augustus and Tiberius who held two and three respectively during their principates (i.e. from 23 BC for Augustus, after the discontinuation of his annual consulships), and these were all to introduce relatives into public life. These four consulships were testimony to Gaius' desire to use his 'full and absolute power' and involve himself in ruling the Empire; he wanted to dominate the senate. He was not only monopolising a consulship that could have been taken up by a senator but also would have instantly shown his intent to govern. Gaius was young and completely lacking experience; he probably felt he had to hold such consulships in order to gain *auctoritas*. Without any political clout, Gaius' position as *princeps*, as first citizen, was completely untenable. Why should the senate be loyal to such a man? Gaius was the first 'unknown quantity' to become emperor, and as such was forced from the beginning into involvement in government in order to validate his position politically. It is no surprise that Gaius attempted a liberal, progressive domestic policy with himself at the helm. Unfortunately for Gaius, by governing so overtly he immediately caused resentment amongst a senate full of men with more political experience, more *auctoritas* and more suitability for government than himself. Gaius had to prove himself to the senate, but by doing so he simply alienated them; he became too popular and soon realised he could act without them, imposing his commands on a body he dominated. His policies would have been more popular with the people than the senate. Gaius took his power seriously, and the government of the Empire. He even joined Corbulo's attack on those incompetents in charge of looking after the roads and fined them. He supposedly even threw mud onto the toga of Vespasian, future emperor, when the latter was aedile, because he was not keeping Rome clean enough.

Where his measures failed (i.e. the restoration of the elections), Gaius showed he was capable of returning to the status quo. His domestic government was not incompetent, and did not have the hallmarks of either a tyrant or madman. It is here we see the hostility of the literary sources. It is strange, considering Gaius' appalling reputation, that we can find little evidence of political incompetence or failed policy on the home front, and there is certainly no evidence of madness. Gaius was not that much more extravagant than his peers, and in any case could afford his policies. These policies were not on the whole to the detriment of Roman society. They were economically sound, in the main popular, and often innovative; many were kept up after his death.

But we do see acts that would have offended a certain rank of Roman, however sound they might have been in their own right. And as we shall see, the one section of Roman society that an emperor could not afford to fall out with was the senate.

# 4

# FOREIGN POLICY

In his short reign Gaius involved himself in many parts of the Empire, but other than his dealings with the Jews and his 'expedition' to Germany and the Dover Straits we have relatively little information about his foreign policy. We must use the same criteria to assess this foreign policy as we did for his internal government; namely, its effectiveness, whether it was consistent with that of his predecessors or whether he innovated successfully, whether his successors kept up such changes, whether his actions were popular, and whether his moves were militarily sound. However, with Gaius' government abroad it is very important to put his policy into context: whether he deviated from Augustus' policy and, if so, whether this caused trouble for the Empire must be investigated. Did Claudius uphold Gaius' modifications?

## PARTHIA

On Gaius' accession Artabanus, the Parthian king, was planning to invade Syria; his hatred of Tiberius was well known. The quick thinking of the Syrian governor, Vitellius, who moved to the Euphrates, overawed the Parthian king. Dio tells us that the two men met and, as Tiberius had just died, Artabanus agreed to pay homage to the son of Germanicus, to the deified Augustus and to the standards. Yet again the reputation of Gaius' father gave him

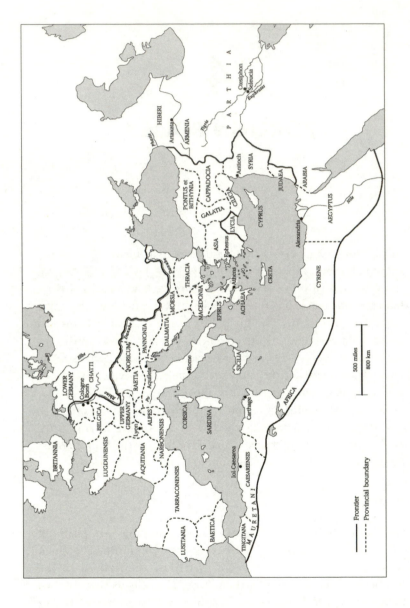

*Figure 2* Map of the Roman Empire in AD 37

an advantage. He gave up Darius – his son – as a hostage. Suetonius tells us: 'Artabanus, for example, king of the Parthians, who was always outspoken in his hatred and contempt for Tiberius, voluntarily sought Gaius' friendship' (*Calig.* 14).

Rome and Parthia had been squabbling over Armenia for years. Tiberius had promoted the pro-Roman Mithridates for the throne of Armenia, following Augustan policy; Gaius recalled and arrested him, which could be seen as possibly part of a bargain with Artabanus. Gaius did not replace him and therefore gave up the Roman attempts to keep Armenia under the rule of a pro-Roman king. This totally contradicted Augustus' policy. He had sent his grandson Gaius Caesar there in 1 BC to insist on Ariobarzanes' rule of Armenia, and Tiberius followed suit with, for example, Germanicus' mission there to crown Artaxias in AD 18. As long as Artaxias survived and Tiberius was strict the arrangement worked. In AD 34 the king's death caused more trouble as Artabanus attempted to put his son Arsaces on the throne while Tiberius was supporting Mithridates. In short, Rome and Parthia were constantly fighting over the candidature for the kingship of Armenia.

Gaius sought a *modus vivendi* with Artabanus straight away; he achieved this. By not sending out a successor to Mithridates he ensured peace in the area. Gaius made sure he was in the driving seat when he 'conceded' Armenia to Parthia because it was done at a time when Parthia was weak (as shown by Artabanus' capitulation to Vitellius) and Rome strong; it was a concession granted and not an arrangement enforced by Parthia. Artabanus had handed over his son as a hostage, and the major threat in the East had been befriended at little cost. There is absolutely no evidence that Armenia was overrun by the Parthians as a consequence. However, Gaius had left Armenia dependent on Parthia. Claudius immediately revoked Gaius' policy and reinstated Mithridates, returning to Augustan and Tiberian precedent. It was this reinstating of Mithridates that caused problems, which resulted in Corbulo's campaigns under Nero. It was arguably only because Gotarzes of Parthia (Artabanus' successor) was so weak that there was no trouble under Claudius. Claudius' attempt to put Meherdates on the throne of Parthia failed. Once Gotarzes had died, and Vologaeses was on the throne, it was a different story; the Parthians pushed Radamistus out of Armenia and this led to war.

The Augustan policy of keeping a ruler of Armenia sympathetic to Rome would obviously have fostered resentment in Parthia, especially as Armenia was so much closer to Parthia in culture and geography. Either a war against Parthia or an abandonment of designs on Armenia would follow. Gaius, or his advisers (Vitellius?) perhaps saw a big campaign in the East as expensive and dangerous. When war finally came under Nero there were massive losses; in AD 66 Tiridates came to Rome to be granted Armenia anyway. Gaius achieved the same through peaceful means as Nero did through a very costly war.

Gaius may have deviated from the Augustan method of keeping face in the area, but he kept the peace by staying on good terms with Artabanus; lives and money were saved. Claudius probably reverted to Augustan precedent only as it seemed the more consistent with Roman honour: the Romans could not be seen to give up and admit defeat. In reality the sensible action was to avoid war. Trade could still continue, and if Gaius did not plan an invasion of Parthia then the strategic positioning of Armenia on its flank was no longer relevant. It was the reversal of Gaius' policy by Claudius that caused a problem. Although by Tiberius' death Artabanus was planning an invasion of Syria, the appointment of Vitellius to the area paid off as it was he who checked the invasion. Gaius pursued a peaceful policy in his reign; under Claudius peace was maintained by virtue of a weak Parthia under Gotarzes. Once Parthia had a stronger ruler, there was war.

Augustus and Tiberius might have turned in their graves at Gaius' policy, but Parthia did not overrun Armenia. What, therefore, was the real loss? Gaius clearly followed a policy of peace in the area from AD 37 to 41, and this was successful. What did Corbulo's campaigns achieve?

## AFRICA

Gaius changed, or began to change, the status of both Africa Proconsularis and Mauretania. In Africa Gaius 'divided the province into two parts, assigning the military force together with the Numidians in its vicinity to another official [i.e. an imperial legate], an arrangement that has continued from that time down to the present' (D.C. 59.20.7). The military garrison would be under an imperial legate, whose *imperium* was dependent on the emperor. There would no longer be a proconsul with independent *imperium* in the area; the senate had lost its last legion.

Dio tells us this was done because Gaius feared Lucius Piso, son of Gnaeus Piso, whose turn it was to govern the province, which held one legion. This smacks of artistic licence; Gnaeus Piso was rumoured to have poisoned Germanicus, and so to Dio it would make a nice coincidence that Gaius feared the son of his father's old enemy. Tacitus has Marcus Silanus as the man to be slighted. The political anomaly of the last legion under a senatorial proconsul would surely have been changed eventually anyway. It made sense, for the emperor's personal security, to have hand-picked imperial legates in control of the army, especially if the emperor was on bad terms with the senate. Whether it was Piso or Silanus who lost out is unimportant; the senate and individual senators lost out. This severely restricted the amount of military commands a senator could enjoy. The change in the African province has been seen as both the first step towards creating Numidia, which was completed under Severus, and a paving of the way for the cultural developments of the second century in North Africa.[1]

The king of Mauretania, Ptolemy, was then called to Rome and executed. There is no credible explanation for this in the sources. Suetonius has his purple cloak angering Gaius so much that Gaius has him executed. Dio gives his standard explanation: Ptolemy was wealthy. Seneca simply attests his death. With both these actions Gaius set in motion the return of Mauretania to the old Republican division into two parts, but now named respectively Mauretania Tingitana and Mauretania Caesariensis (Pliny *H.N.* 5.2; Dio ascribes the change to Claudius in 60.9.5). In early AD 40 there was a revolt under Aedemon of the Mauri, although it was not necessarily due to Ptolemy's death as Ptolemy had not been popular with all his peoples. Claudius put this down by AD 42 and maintained the division of the province into two parts. Tiberius had left Ptolemy alone in Mauretania, but his poor performance in dealing with Tacfarinas' revolt in AD 17, which was finally put down only in AD 24 by Blaesus, showed how exposed Africa Proconsularis was on its western boundary.[2] Therefore it made sense strategically to incorporate Mauretania; there were a number of Roman colonies there that also needed protection. By AD 43 Claudius had completed the incorporation and division of Mauretania, and it was clearly sound policy.

Without speculating too much on Gaius' fear of provincial governors (i.e. Piso, or Ptolemy's links with Gaetulicus and arrest at the time of his plot), we may wonder why Gaius set the wheels in motion for the military reconstruction of Africa and the incorporation of Mauretania, which deprived the senate of its last legion. Did it make sense as a policy?

The upshot of both these changes was a revolt, possibly due to the incorporation of Mauretania and loss of their king; but not all the Mauretanian communities were involved – many of those communities had disliked Ptolemy. If the peace was to be maintained in North Africa, Mauretania could not remain independent; the safety of the province of Africa required a change. There seems to have been minimal disruption involved in changing Africa Proconsularis; Gaius could have taken it from the senate completely. Garzetti is surely too harsh when he talks of Mauretania being left in tatters on Gaius' death as he had not suggested any successor to Ptolemy.[3] Any changes of this sort would incur opposition; more importantly, the revolt was swiftly put down. From then on the security of the area was increased.

Even under Augustus there had been intermittent fighting as Juba II continually asked for Roman assistance; Gaius took measures to stop such trouble. The decision, surely based on military requirements, was kept up by his successors, who would have also felt safer without any senators having independent *imperium*. Yet again, the only section of Roman society which would have been angered by Gaius' actions was the senate. As we do not know the reasons behind Ptolemy's death, we have to look at this measure in its own terms. Gaius secured the area as an act of foreign policy while following the Augustan precedent of incorporation, and not by the use of client kings, the latter of which was Gaius' preferred method as we will now see.

## COMMAGENE

Antiochus IV received his father's old kingdom of Commagene from Gaius, and supposedly 100 million sesterces along with it. Although we should not trust the amount too much, we have an example of Gaius acting generously towards client kings. Since AD 17 Commagene had been a Roman province; Gaius was again moving away from Tiberius' policy. By AD 69 Antiochus was reported to be the richest client king. Gaius ensured his loyalty and gratitude by his benevolence; Claudius again kept up Gaius' appointment. Antiochus IV had links with Agrippa and was present in Gaul with him; it is possible he dedicated the city Germanicopolis to Gaius. (Dio is surely confused when he speaks of Gaius deposing Antiochus after giving him Commagene.)

## THRACE

Similarly, Gaius treated the three Thracian princes, sons of Cotys, well. They had grown up with him in Rome as in AD 19 Tiberius had seen them as too young to rule after the death of their father, sending the governor Rufus to their provinces instead; this had led to uprisings in AD 21 and 26. Dio tells us that the younger Cotys received Lesser Armenia, Rhoemetalces received the possessions of the elder Cotys (i.e. his father's dominions in Thrace) and Polemo II received his 'ancestral domain' (i.e. probably Pontus), 'all upon the vote of the senate' (59.12.2). There was a lavish ceremony in the Forum for the princes and Gaius' generosity sealed their friendship.

Polemo II proved loyal and helped in Corbulo's campaign against Parthia. Cotys held his kingdom throughout Claudius' reign and neither rebelled nor caused trouble. However, Claudius annexed Thrace in AD 46 despite the loyalty of Rhoemetalces. This led to fierce resistance, and only from AD 61 was Thrace truly obedient. Again, during Gaius' lifetime none of the three princes caused any trouble; they had been educated with Gaius and were bound to him. Although Augustus and Tiberius had headed away from client kings, Augustus had promised Polemo I of Pontus the Bosporan kingdom. As Gaius probably gave Polemo II Pontus (and possibly the Bosporan area), he was acting under Augustan precedent. It shows that Augustus was willing to use client kings if he thought it necessary. Claudius granted Mithridates, whom Gaius had imprisoned, the Bosporus area.

## GAUL

Gaius fostered loyalty in the provinces by visiting Gaul and holding auctions and an oratory contest at Lugdunum. Some of the Gallic provinces had revolted in AD 21 and Tiberius had supposedly promised to go to Gaul but never did. Julius and Augustus had laid the foundations for the development of Gallo-Roman culture but Tiberius had simply left the Gauls alone. Gaius personally encouraged the provincials by, for example, letting Gauls into the equestrian order. Tiberius had not taken pains to promote provincials, while Gaius encouraged them to strive for the citizenship and for their elites to move into politics; Philo mentions a letter where Gaius promises citizenship to certain cities. This can be seen as another progressive move and an advance in the social history of the Empire. The road building that Tiberius had maintained also continued under Gaius in Gaul (as well as in Illyricum and Spain), as attested by milestones.

## ITALY

It was not just Gaul that received Gaius' attentions; Gaius also visited various parts of Italy other than his base in Rome. On Drusilla's death Gaius went around Campania and Sicily. Similarly, his building programme continued beyond the Straits of Messina, as did his enthusiasm for shows; a festival was given at Syracuse and the walls and temple there were repaired.

## GERMANY AND BRITAIN

The madness that surrounds Gaius is ever present here in the ancient sources' depictions of his German campaign and 'attempted invasion' of Britain. There are no contemporary sources on the subject. Seneca and Pliny the Elder do not mention the expedition and so we are left with Suetonius, Dio and a few words in Tacitus.

We have already seen how unreliable both Suetonius and Dio are; their accounts make little sense here. Both give, yet again, trivial reasons for the expedition, Suetonius (*Calig.* 43) tells us it was 'unpremeditated' and that Gaius attempted the expedition

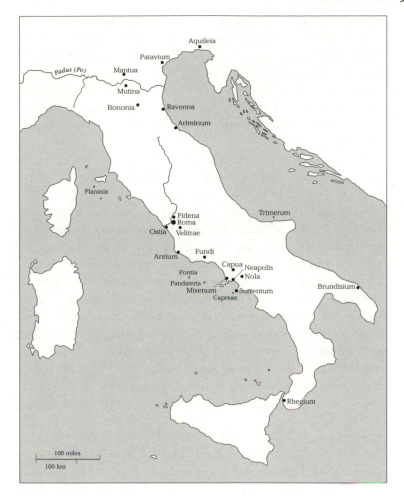

*Figure 3* Map of Italy

because while at the sacred grove of Bevagna he was told to recruit more Batavians for his bodyguard. Dio states that he undertook the campaign in order to exploit the wealth of Gaul and Spain, and then has Gaius setting out a short distance across the Rhine before turning back to conduct a campaign against Britain. They both agree that he left without warning and marched incredibly quickly northwards (so quick the standards of the praetorians had to be carried on pack animals and water was sprinkled on the roads ahead of the column to ease the march). Yet we are also told of Gaius 'holding levies everywhere with the utmost strictness' (Suet. *Calig.* 43), and Dio states that he had gathered 200,000 or 250,000 men. Even here we have a contradiction: the expedition was on a whim and speedily done and yet the sheer logistics of such an operation would have required massive preparations and some sort of planning.

We must look at the events in light of the hostile sources, who seem to do their best to mock the expedition. Here are these events as depicted in the two main sources.

Suetonius tells us that once the army reached 'camp', presumably near the Rhine, Gaius dismissed any generals who had been late in bringing auxiliaries and discharged many veterans for both age and incapacity, scaling down their retirement bonus; 'all that he accomplished was to receive the surrender of Adminius' (*Calig.* 44). Despatches were sent to the senate as if Britain had been conquered. He then 'had a few Germans from those in captivity taken across the river and concealed there, and word brought him after lunch with great bustle and confusion that the enemy were close at hand' (*Calig.* 45). He continued to charge after them and then returned, giving some of his men a ranger's crown. 'Another time some hostages were taken from a primary school and secretly sent on ahead of him.' He also caught these. 'Finally, as if he intended to bring the war to an end, he drew up a line of battle on the shore of the Ocean, arranging his ballistas and other artillery' (*Calig.* 46). He then ordered the soldiers to pick up shells, calling them 'spoils from the Ocean, due to the Capitol and Palatine'. He erected a lighthouse, gave his soldiers one hundred *denarii* each and even added some Gauls dressed as Germans 'in addition to a few captives and deserters from the native tribes' (*Calig.* 47). This is followed with the ridiculous claim that Gaius then attempted to massacre the legions that had mutinied in AD 14. When they noticed what he was doing, they went for their arms and Gaius ran away!

Dio's account is equally odd. Gaius conducted the campaign 'ostensibly because the hostile Germans were stirring up trouble', but in reality to raise money (D.C. 59.21.2). He took with him women, actors and gladiators and made haste north. Dio tells us that he did no harm to the enemy. He simply crossed the Rhine a little way, returned and 'then set out as if to conduct a campaign against Britain, but turned back from the ocean's edge, showing no little vexation at his lieutenants who won some slight successes' (59.21.3). Dio goes on to say that he inflicted vast ills on his allies instead. Dio (59.21.4) sees Gaius auctioning off imperial property. 'He murdered some men on the ground that they were rebelling and others on the ground that they were conspiring against him', but the real reason was for their wealth. Again, in D.C. 59.22.2 he states there was no battle and no enemy slain except some caught by a 'ruse'. Gaetulicus was killed 'for the reason that he was endeared to the soldiers' (D.C. 59.22.5). To celebrate Lepidus' death Gaius gave the soldiers money. Dio even has Gaius telling the senate he had escaped a great plot. Dio even tries to belittle this by saying Gaius was always pretending to be in danger. Dio then returns to events on the ocean's edge and describes Gaius drawing up his soldiers on a beach, embarking on a trireme, returning, placing himself on a lofty platform and then giving the order to pick up shells. 'Having secured these spoils (for he needed booty, of course, for his triumphal procession) he became greatly elated, as if he had enslaved the very ocean; and he gave his soldiers many presents' (D.C. 59.25.3).

There are similarities in the two sources: both agree the march north was in haste, both show the campaign as a farce and mention the punishment of certain people. Importantly, both claim nothing major was achieved.

Scholars have put forward many views on what really happened and why the bizarre 'campaign' was planned at all.[4] There are certain facts which set an important backdrop for the expedition to the Rhine. Prestige on the Rhine had continued to be low since the time of Varus' defeat under Augustus. Then, during the reign of Tiberius, the governor of the Upper Rhine, Gaetulicus, let things slip. The German tribes were making inroads into Gaul and Gaetulicus could not control the aggressive German incursions. In AD 39 there was a danger that the whole of the south of Britain under Verica could be overrun by anti-Roman forces, and so it was a strategic time for action in both areas. An aggressive frontier policy against Germany with a view to securing the area would pave the way for an invasion of Britain by securing its flank. The situation on the Rhine was bad anyway, and needed attention. So, were there extensive preparations or was the march north conducted on a whim? Evidence suggests that the two legions XV and XXII Primigeniae were raised during the reign of Gaius; they were used early in Claudius' reign to hold the Rhine frontier while the more established legions invaded Britain. Galba was involved in the training of 'new recruits' – presumably those legions Gaius raised (Suet. *Galb.* 6). There is also evidence that detachments from XXII Deiotariana, III Cyrenaica and IV Macedonica were also present on the Rhine.[5] All this suggests massive preparations; if these legions were raised by Gaius then the operation certainly had purpose. The famous bridge of boats at Baiae could then be seen in the light of inspiring fear into both Germany and Britain, as Suetonius mentions. Moreover, there is evidence of a Gaian legionary base at Weisenau, and a tombstone from XV Primigenia in the area does point to preparations of some kind. On the assumption, therefore, that the Roman war machine had been put into full swing, befitting an expedition in the presence of the emperor himself, why was there such a sudden departure? This could be explained by Gaius stumbling across the plot of Gaetulicus and Lepidus; Gaius had to act quickly to avoid suspicion and could not postpone his operation as this might let the Germans gain confidence. This would also go some way to explaining not only the size of the force taken (Dio would have us believe 200,000–250,000 men) but also why Gaius felt the need to bring his praetorian guard with him. If Gaetulicus was so popular among the ranks, then regaining loyalty in the area would not be easy.

Suetonius does not even mention a conspiracy in his *Life of Gaius*, and it is perhaps a slip when he does so in *Claudius* 9 where he refers to the plot of 'Lepidus and Gaetulicus'. Perhaps this silence was to mock Gaius. Similarly, Dio's reason for the death of Gaetulicus also plays down his possible role in a conspiracy, but still hints at it: he lost his life 'for the reason he was endeared to the soldiers'. Dio goes too far when he claims Gaius 'was always pretending to be in danger' (59.23.1). Considering the sources' hostility to Gaius, talk of an actual conspiracy, however hidden, should be accepted as fact. Such a plot would explain perfectly why Gaius moved so quickly, why he took his praetorian cohorts with him and why he brought his sisters along. The praetorians acted as a powerful bodyguard, while the inclusion of his sisters meant he could keep an eye on them. Both Agrippina and Livilla were later banished for involvement in a plot.

At any rate, a huge force went to the Rhine and arrested the 'conspirators'; what follows sounds like Galba's attempts to get the Rhine armies into shape. Many centurions and generals were discharged for incompetence and perhaps even disloyalty. As descriptions of battles, the sources do not really make sense, and so many have seen the expedition as trying to push out the barbarian incursions and then oversee troop manoeuvres in order to regain some loyalty. And so the accounts of the sources have been seen as describing war games or drills. Barrett still thinks a campaign against the Germans was possible; he sees the propaganda surrounding the undertaking, Tacitus' reference to the 'massive efforts against Germany' (*Agr.* 13) and the evidence for resistance from the Caninefates as proof of this. It is true that Suetonius tells us that Galba 'speedily checked the barbarians, who had already made inroads even into Gaul' (*Galb.* 6); this is in direct contradiction to the farce he gives us in his *Life of Gaius*. Galba was still fighting the Chatti in AD 41 after Gaius' death, and so there must have been prolonged fighting and frontier strengthening. Barrett sees Gaius leaving Italy in the autumn, staying at Lyons until Galba could secure the frontier and appearing on that frontier in a carefully stage-managed affair, like Claudius in Britain in AD 43. (A relief at Koula in Lydia – *I.L.S.* 8791 – shows a Roman cavalryman pointing a spear at a cowering Germania from Gaius's reign.) The sources do say Gaius crossed the Rhine, even if they try to discredit him for having done so.

Gaius was the first emperor to represent imperial speeches to the army on coins, emphasising his connection to the army, and he also adopted the title 'Father of the Armies' and took command of the Rhine legions. His nickname would also have endeared him to the soldiers. If Gaius sought the reputation of a tough general, the hostile sources have done their best to depict such actions as farce. This is exemplified by Dio's mockery of Gaius, saying he was hailed *imperator* seven times, which he later contradicts when talking about Claudius. There is no inscriptional or numismatic evidence for such a salute and yet it would have been an ideal subject matter for coinage. It was the first time the emperor had been on campaign with the troops for 50 years, and so a natural time for them to salute him.

Whatever actually happened on the Rhine we should be wary of the unintelligible accounts of the sources, with their anecdotes of picking up shells and attempts to massacre his own legions, and instead try to see what Gaius actually achieved there. He left the Rhine frontier secure in Galba's hands, having fortified it and stopped the barbarian incursions. He left a more loyal army on the Rhine, and had restored discipline. The donative to the troops could easily have been for loyalty after the conspiracy and deaths of Gaetulicus and Lepidus. The conspirators had been killed and the men who were below par weeded out. Had there been many Roman casualties in all this, the hostile sources would have mentioned them, so we can assume this was achieved with minimal loss. As we do not know the aims of Gaius or his commanding officers it is hard to judge its success, but looking at the area before and after Gaius' visit it is evident he achieved a lot. The anecdotes of trapping his own men, running away at the first sign of the enemy and dressing up Gauls as Germans are highly unlikely when one looks at the context of the passages. If Gaius had campaigned with such ineptitude and not only insulted the soldiers by commanding them to pick up shells but also attempted the massacre of his own men, having just killed a very popular commander for no good reason other than his popularity, then surely Gaius would not have come back from the north alive – such a version of events is ridiculous. Manoeuvres probably were carried out to drill the troops, but whether we should try to explain the sources' confused accounts in these terms (as certain scholars would) is questionable. The interpretation of Gaius' military policy in the area is so partisan that the accounts barely make sense at all.

Even without the conspiracy of Gaetulicus and Lepidus, or the threat of a revolt similar to that which Germanicus suppressed in AD 14, Gaius still had a reason to travel. Putting aside Gaius' own natural desire for military glory (something which he had no experience in, unlike his predecessors, and which was probably necessary for his own *auctoritas*) and his father's reputation with the Rhine legions, not to mention the family name Germanicus, the facts seem to give a perfectly valid reason for going: the Rhine frontier simply was not secure. Moreover, it had suffered from lack of interest on the part of Tiberius who retired to Capreae and left his provincial governors to deal with their territories. Gaetulicus' laziness and length of command were direct products of Tiberius' lack of interest in the Empire in his later reign. Gaius, far from attempting to conquer more German territory and failing, kept up his predecessors' policy on the Rhine. Once Varus' legions had been lost in AD 9, Augustus gave up on an Elbe frontier and seemed happy to secure the Rhine. Of course, to do this necessitated punitive expeditions over the river to lay waste the enemies' territories and ensure they were kept at arm's length. Tiberius had taken eight legions across after Varus' defeat and had done just that. Such measures not only secured the area but also raised morale.

Similarly, when the German legions revolted on Augustus' death, Germanicus took them over the Rhine to restore discipline and morale as he did in AD 14. When Germanicus seemed to be attempting a more offensive policy he was duly recalled by Tiberius, who took Augustus' advice and did not aim at an expansion of the Empire. Tiberius' own time in Germany would have taught him that advancing too far without consolidating the gains was disastrous.

Gaius' actions on the Rhine, pieced together from what we can trust in the sources, are entirely consistent with such measures. Gaius reorganised the command, sacking incompetents, and secured the area to stop barbarian incursions; we are told of no casualties. If Gaius had attempted a serious offensive to gain territory, perhaps up to the Elbe, then there would have been many. Instead he continued the defensive policy of his predecessors, which necessitated small-scale forays over the Rhine and laying waste the area, while at the same time restoring morale; Galba was certainly a good appointment to the Upper Rhine. In fact, just as Germanicus had expelled the Chatti from their homeland, Galba achieved a victory against them in AD 41 after Gaius' death – a measure necessary to secure the frontier. Similarly, in the same year Publius Gabinius Secundus undertook an expedition against the Chauci. Under Gaius' successor this defensive policy was continued. Claudius recalled Corbulo, who was about to cross the Rhine and fight the Chauci, and favoured the defensive stance too.

In short, Gaius made preparations for later successes on the Rhine, and there were few casualties in the operations to expel the barbarians which secured the frontier and regained the loyalty of the Rhine armies. Securing the frontier and raising two new legions paved the way for Claudius' successful invasion of Britain, and it is to the confused accounts in the sources of Gaius' exploits on the Dover Straits that we must now turn.

From Germany Gaius went to the shore of the Channel. What he was doing there has been the topic of debate for some time, with various scholars putting forward opinions. Amongst them are the following explanations for the non-implementation of the invasion: either the troops mutinied on the shore, and Gaius made them pick up shells as humiliation, or the tradition of the soldiers picking up shells comes from a misunderstanding of the term *musculi* (a technical term for sappers' huts), or Gaius found the Rhine army in such poor discipline that he cancelled the proposed invasion. The intended assault has been seen as postponed because of the plot of Gaetulicus and a distinct lack of discipline. Some historians feel an invasion was never planned at all as the troops had not been drilled enough and it was far too early in the season to cross the Channel safely, and they point to the fact that there is no mention of transport ships in the sources. However, there is a similar silence on the subject when the sources describe Claudius' invasion of Britain. Explanations for the shell incident have included the shells being used to simulate missile fire during a mock landing, which may explain the artillery being drawn up, but is thoroughly unconvincing.

Bicknell strongly argues the case for the events not actually occurring on the Channel at all, but his conclusion – that legions I and XX showed cowardice on the Rhine, were made to pick up shells as punishment, and that then Gaius contemplated decimation but instead gave them a donative and had them construct a lighthouse – simply does not add up.[6] A donative is hardly appropriate for legions Gaius sought to decimate. And the donative was not as pitiful as Bicknell makes out; it was around a third of the foot soldier's annual wages. Surely an attempt at decimation would have caused a massive revolt in such circumstances. If a

similar mutiny took place on the shore, would Gaius really provoke them by ordering them to pick up shells to insult them;
Gaius had just had their favoured commander killed and would be
playing with fire.

Here it would be folly to follow the confused (and incomplete
in the case of Dio) accounts of the hostile sources too readily. It is
possible that a hostile tradition downplays the link between the
Channel events and the receiving of the British prince Adminius;
Suetonius only glances over the achievement briefly and Dio does
not mention the prince at all. The reception of Adminius would
explain the military pomp and the donative given to the soldiers;
they had been involved in a piece of ceremonial that declared
Gaius' intention to invade Britain. He possibly intended to install
Adminius on the throne and received him in a ceremony of sorts.
The collection of shells was simply a part of that ceremony.
Suetonius even tells us 'all that he accomplished was the surrender
of Adminius' (*Calig.* 44). Therefore this must have been seen as a
diplomatic victory of some sort.

Both sources show confused chronology and so we simply know
that Gaius led an army north, foiled a conspiracy and strength-
ened the Rhine frontier. This can well be seen as a precursor to an
invasion of Britain, but it does not mean the invasion was planned
for the spring of AD 40. It could just have been part of a slow
military process, to be completed whenever the opportunity arose.
This theory ties in with Tacitus' explanation that Gaius did not
invade because 'his massive efforts against Germany had failed'
(*Agr.* 13); that is, Galba was still fighting the Chatti in AD 41 and
so the flank was not secure for an invasion into Britain when Gaius
was alive. The opportunity had not yet arisen, but two legions
were being trained so that they would be ready for such an occurrence. The events on the coast have been explained in a number of
ways, but both the explanations of Suetonius and Dio suffice when
talking of the shells; they were taken for his triumph and for the
Capitol and Palatine. If Adminius had arrived when Gaius was
on the Rhine, Gaius might have decided to receive him officially
on the coast in a ceremony. And where better than on a trireme on
the ocean in full sight of his army – a sight that would impress
Adminius? The sources' narration of the coastal events smack of
pomp and ceremony. Gaius was celebrating the 'surrender' of

Adminius, perhaps promising to instate him as client king of the island once he had invaded. Kentish coins of the time had his name (Amminus) on them; Gaius' ceremony was celebrated with a donative to the troops. A despatch to the senate talking of his foiling of Gaetulicus' conspiracy and his receiving of Adminius would make perfect sense. Gaius could look forward to a triumph at home celebrating these two 'victories', and he had the shells and the trireme he used to meet Adminius taken home for that triumph.

Military activity has always been a target for hostile sources.[7] Trajan was not castigated much for his failure in the East because he was liked by the senate, and senators wrote history; in the case of Gaius the sources are so confused and full of unintelligible anecdotes that are probably mocking a rather mundane, almost dull reality. There was no massive victory or defeat to talk of. Gaius' formal acceptance of Britain was a commitment that Claudius took seriously; he invaded in AD 43. Surely this is testimony to Gaius' preparations; the legions would have needed time to prepare and yet were ready very early in Claudius' reign.

There are some scholars who accept the sources too readily. Ferrill, for example, accepts Dio's chronology and claims we should not attempt to rationalise the actions of a madman.[8] If the emperor really was losing his grip and behaved with the random acts depicted by the sources, the troops would have rebelled there and then. We must surely dismiss Gaius' attempts at decimation as ridiculous. If Gaius really had been forced to flee from the legions this would have spelt grave danger for the emperor's regime. In fact, this story could have come from a further misconception of manoeuvres and tactics training: rangers would attempt to creep up on victims in an ambush or mock ambush.

Gaius left the north not only having secured the Rhine armies, and frontier, but also having personally seen his troops, fostering loyalty and making way for a successful invasion of Britain that in the end occurred after his death. The sources are full of what Gaius planned to do. When we look at what he did we can survey how practical and almost mundane his policy was. The sources do not talk of any Roman casualties and, as hostile as they are, this would surely have been picked up on if true, so Gaius achieved all this without setbacks. It is possible that his experience of AD 14 and the mutiny of the Rhine armies, and what he was told about it by his father, meant he feared such trouble again; hence his intervention with a strong force and his taking of the praetorian guard with him.

There is much evidence here for a sound military policy; there was no catastrophe and Gaius prepared the imperial army for a victory both against the Chatti in AD 41 and in Britain in AD 43. Augustus had never dismissed the invasion of Britain – poetry from his early career is full of such planned endeavours. Britain certainly held a place in the heart of the Roman people, and it would be the perfect way to outdo one's predecessors and continue the precedent set by Julius Caesar, thus gaining popularity. Gaius merely lived too short a time to put his plans into practice.

Claudius refused to hand Adminius back to Britain, and war was declared; Claudius was also an emperor in need of military glory. The fact that Adminius fled from Britain shows that the anti-Roman party had gained the upper hand in the territory of Cunobelinus, a circumstance which simply adds to the reasons for an invasion. Claudius' advisers, like Seneca, pushed for such an invasion; it is therefore possible that Gaius' advisers had been giving similar advice.

Treating with due circumspection the ridiculous interpretations of Gaius' actions in the sources, and simply looking at the probable order of events, we see a policy on the Rhine that was continuous with both those of his predecessors and successor – and practical. Similarly, the invasion of Britain which Gaius initiated not only had precedent in the actions of Julius Caesar but was also an aim of Augustus. Claudius finished Gaius' work.

Instead of farce, we find a sensible and simple foreign policy in Gaius' actions with both the Germans and Britons.


## THE JEWS

Neither Suetonius nor Dio mentions Gaius' dealings with the Jews, and so we have to rely on the Jewish sources with their obvious bias.[9] (See Appendix 1.) Bearing each source and each source's background in mind, we must look at what they say happened under Gaius.

## Judaea

One of Gaius' first moves as *princeps* was to free Herod Agrippa, imprisoned by Tiberius, and give him 'kingship over that third part of his grandfather's [King Herod] territory, the revenues of which were taken by Philip the tetrarch, Agrippa's paternal uncle' (Ph. *In Flacc.* 25; see also J. *A.J.* 18.194, 237; D.C. 59.8.2). From 4 BC the area had been controlled by an ethnarch; Gaius not only gave them a king but also gave that king the *ornamenta praetoria* (the first time that the honour had been bestowed on a king). Although this did not confer any actual power, it was indicative of the emperor's favour. Agrippa had been in the royal court when Gaius was growing up, and the two were obviously on good terms. Having such a friend on the throne of a subject territory held obvious advantages: it lessened the chance of hostility.

Augustus, in AD 6, had banished Archelaus and taken his territory (Judaea proper, Samaria and Idumaea) into the province of Judaea. On Philip's death, Tiberius had placed his dominion (i.e. Trachonitis, Gaulanitis and the Batanean tribe) under the authority of the governor of Syria, with its revenues kept in a separate fund; Gaius yet again moved away from this policy of incorporation to put Agrippa on the throne. Claudius kept this appointment; it was sensible to keep such a loyal client king in place. But, on Agrippa's death in AD 44, Agrippa II was only 16 and his territory became a province again. Under Claudius the province saw a string of ignorant governors who soured the relations between the Jews and Romans. We will now deal with the Jews, but just because Gaius' policy was different from that of his predecessors does not make it bad policy; Agrippa proved a good appointment and was instrumental in resolving the problem over Gaius' supposed proposal for a statue, as we will now see.

## The disturbance in Alexandria

Philo's *In Flaccum* has Flaccus, the prefect of Egypt, worried for his future on Gaius' accession because 'he had been a devoted partisan of the actual [Tiberius Gemellus] rather than the adopted [grand]

children [of Tiberius] . . . Or again as he had been one of those
who had attacked Gaius' mother' (*In Flacc.* 9, 10). He had also
been friendly with Macro. Greek nationalists, namely Isidorus and
Lampon, offered Flaccus protection from Gaius in exchange for his
support for their actions: they wanted him to turn a blind eye to
their bullying of the Jews of Alexandria. Flaccus agreed, unrest
ensued in Alexandria, and scenes of carnage followed. Eventually
Flaccus was arrested by Gaius and the violence ended. Here
the Greeks obviously resented the Jewish residents of the city:
Agrippa's visit as their king annoyed the Greeks, and Flaccus
could not control the situation. Gaius is seen only as the saviour of
the Jews, as he was the messenger of God's will.

The *Legatio* gives a completely different story. Because of the
disruption in Alexandria, two embassies were sent to Gaius to ask
for help by both the Jews under Philo and the Greeks under
Apion and Isidorus. A summary of Gaius' reign is given towards
the beginning of the *Legatio* which highlights Gaius' madness and
tyrannical rule. The work does not give the resolution of the
Alexandrian troubles. The reception of the Jewish embassy is
depicted as a sham; Gaius mocked the Jews and claimed he was a
god. Josephus simply speaks of a tumult in Alexandria leading to
the Jewish embassy.

There was a clear Greek nationalism growing in Alexandria
under demagogues like Isidorus: in short, the unrest of AD 38
would have happened regardless of emperor. It is, after all, too
early in Gaius' reign to ascribe the cause of such civil unrest to
him. Greek-Jewish antagonism was an age-old phenomenon at
the time in all the cities where Jews and gentiles lived together.
The events at Jamnia show it was not just Alexandria that saw
urban unrest. Perhaps Flaccus' fear of Gaius did lead him to find
refuge in the anti-Jewish quarters of Alexandria, but the trouble
was in no way down to Gaius. Moreover, Philo gives no account
of the situation in the city at the time; there was a background of
social and political problems between the Jews and Greeks of
Alexandria.

Evidence points to the embassy to Gaius requesting participation in the Greek citizenship of Alexandria for the Jewish people
of the city. Since Bell's publication of Claudius' letter to the
Alexandrians, most scholars believe that the Jews did not enjoy

this citizenship and were requesting it at their embassy to Gaius. This would explain Claudius' words to the Jews of Alexandria not to strive for any more rights than they already had.[10] The unrest in Alexandria can therefore be viewed in the light of Jewish desire for more rights, and Greek resentment thereof. Philo keeps quiet on the subject to portray his people in a better light. This fact of concern over citizenship is also backed up by Flaccus calling the Jews 'foreigners' (Ph. *In. Flacc.* 172): Smallwood claims that, as Philo was intending to show Flaccus' crimes, he would have shown if Flaccus was insulting citizens as this would have made his crimes greater.[11]

Agrippa's tactless visit to Alexandria enhanced the disturbance, showing the Greeks that the Jews had a powerful ally in their king who was a personal friend to the emperor himself. The embassy would not have been sent if the Jews either thought Gaius was insane or in some way blamed him for Flaccus' actions. On the contrary, their embassy shows their belief and hope in their emperor. Philo's picture of the ridiculous reception they got cannot fully be believed; they were heard and they all lived to tell the tale. We will never know the actual words spoken, but we must be sceptical about those Philo gives us. Gaius died before his answer was given; Claudius dealt with the embassy and the citizenship issue.

Flaccus was recalled and replaced and the trouble died down in Alexandria. Barrett has pointed out that one year later the Jews of the city had so much returned to normal that they could afford a hecatomb to Gaius for success in Germany.[12] Perhaps Philo's talk of the brutality and destructiveness of the riot was exaggerated. Moreover, Jewish attacks on the Greeks in AD 41 under Claudius may make the passive part the Jews played in the trouble under Flaccus unlikely. The governor did arrest 38 members of the Jewish senate; he also searched the Jewish quarter for weapons. These events are evidence of possible Jewish resistance. In short, Gaius' recall of Flaccus ended the unrest, regardless of whether he was recalled for misadministration or because of his ties with Macro and Gemellus. Gaius' dealings with the Jews of Alexandria was sound. It is the order for his statue that has to be looked at to see if there is evidence of incompetence in his foreign policy concerning the Jews.

## The order for the statue

It was in Italy that the embassy found out that Gaius was planning to place his statue in the temple at Jerusalem, in response to
the pulling down of an imperial altar at Jamnia by the Jews. Philo
goes on to explain the reasons for Gaius' order to erect the statue
as also because the Jews would not honour him as a god, and that
his policy was on the advice of Apelles, Helicon and other enemies
of the Jews. Gaius waged again 'a vast and truceless war' against
the Jews (*Leg.* 119), and Petronius was ordered to use two
legions to set up the statue. Massive demonstrations followed, and
Petronius wrote to Gaius explaining the situation – a revolt could
occur, and the Jews were failing to till the land, which could have
led to a famine. Herod Agrippa, in Rome, fainted on hearing news
of Gaius' plan, and wrote Gaius a letter begging him to
reconsider. Gaius did reconsider, but, on hearing Petronius' news
and reluctance to carry out his emperor's command, he ordered
Petronius' suicide. Philo claims Gaius planned a second statue but
died before he could go ahead with his evil scheme. A short aside
is also given on the demise of Apelles and Helicon, also at the
hands of God.

Josephus' *Bellum Judaicum* gives only a brief outline of events,
in which Gaius decided to proclaim his own divinity by erecting
his statue at Jerusalem. He told Petronius to put 'the recalcitrants
to death and to reduce the whole nation to slavery' (*B.J.* 185) if
anyone opposed his move. Demonstrations followed, Petronius
wrote to Gaius explaining the situation, but Gaius was
unimpressed and ordered his suicide. God killed off Gaius, and
delayed the message of death for Petronius – the reward for his
defence of the Jewish people.

The *Antiquitates* of Josephus expands on this; the situation in
Alexandria led to the embassy to Gaius where Apion fulminated
against the Jews – Gaius was so annoyed at not being called a god
by the Jews that he ordered his statue for their temple at Jerusalem.
In *A.J.* 18.263 Petronius met massive demonstrations by the
people, followed by the qualms of the elders at a meeting in
Tiberias. The Jews went on strike, refusing to till the land and
collect fruits, and Petronius wrote to Gaius. Meanwhile, at a
banquet held for Gaius by Agrippa, Agrippa was promised a

favour, and asked Gaius not to put up his statue. Gaius agreed, ordered Petronius to halt, but later got Petronius' original letter. Angered, he ordered Petronius' suicide but died before his orders could be carried out.

A close analysis of all four works by the two authors shows many contradictions, but agreement roughly on the main events. The interpretations and explanations may be widely different, but each individual source 'lets slip' pieces of information that perhaps the other was on purpose leaving out. The result is various interpretations of the project. The confusion in the sources, and absence of the statue in certain works, raises the question: was there such an order for a statue at all?

Josephus, in *Bellum Judaicum*, has Gaius' proclamation of his divinity as the simple reason behind the plan for the statue; *A.J.* 18.261 agrees: 'indignant at being so slighted by the Jews alone, Gaius dispatched Petronius as his Legate' to set up the statue. Philo's *Legatio* gives three reasons for Gaius' decision to set up his statue: the Jews would not honour Gaius as a god, a reaction to Jamnia, and on the advice of Helicon and Apelles. Without the *Legatio* the only reason for the statue – Gaius' belief in his own divinity – shows Gaius up as ludicrous or even mad. But if it is seen as a reaction (over-reaction) to the pulling down of an imperial altar at Jamnia it makes a lot more sense.

Petronius is a much more important figure in Philo. In the *Legatio* he was slow to act from the beginning, seeing the inappropriateness of the action. Josephus says he hurried to his duties. Josephus changes Petronius' character; Philo even has him understanding Jewish philosophy. Although Petronius' movements with his two legions and the demonstrating Jews do differ drastically in each source, both writers agree that he wrote to Gaius having spoken to the Jews personally.

Philo, in the *Legatio*, has Agrippa, the Jews of the embassy and the Jews of Palestine all surprised at Gaius' actions: Agrippa fainted, the Jews of the delegation stood 'speechless and powerless' (189), and the Jews of Palestine stood rooted to the ground. The similarities between the reactions have been pointed out by Bilde[13] and show artistic licence. This treatment of Agrippa also contradicts Josephus' portrayal of the king, where he is closer to Gaius and friendlier with him.

Both accounts do have Agrippa intervening, and ultimately stopping the statue, but they both play this down. Josephus, in *Bellum Judaicum*, avoids mentioning Agrippa. In *A.J.* 18.301 he has Gaius angry with Petronius' letter and says that Gaius 'concluded that the Jews were bent on revolt'. Philo has Gaius planning a second statue, and so Agrippa's achievement is again hidden.

Per Bilde goes on to explain that Philo's literary conception of Gaius did not allow a realistic description of him; the missing palinode which could have had in it a discussion of Gaius' death, as most scholars believe, would have required divine intervention, and this in turn would have required Gaius to go back on his word.[14] Philo also has Sejanus' supposed anti-Jewish policy being halted by his death.

Although we should treat Gaius' supposed plans with scepticism and concentrate on events, as Petronius seems to have moved troops and met resistance, this order for the statue must be looked into. We must remember, however, that no such statue was ever set up and the hostile sources make the most of a command from Gaius that may never have been implemented or possibly ordered at all. Gaius' plans for a statue had precedent in the exploits of Antiochus IV who in 167 BC set up his own altars in synagogues across Judaea. Philo would have known of this as he would have had access to the Book of Maccabees, and his writings on the Alexandrian trouble show other similarities – that is, in the enforced eating of pork. Was Philo merely bringing his knowledge of history to bear and exaggerating the events of both the disturbances and the order for a statue in the temple?

Among the reasons given for Gaius' order was that on reading of the tearing down of an imperial altar at Jamnia, Gaius 'gave orders that in place of the altar of bricks erected [by the Greeks] in wanton spite in Jamnia something richer and more magnificent, namely a colossal statue coated with gold, should be set up in the temple of the mother city' (Ph. *Leg.* 203).

Superficially this may seem a massive over-reaction by a man vain enough to care that some Jewish inhabitants of Jamnia would not honour him as a god. But the desecration of the altar at Jamnia could be seen as a political act. The imperial cult represented Rome, and attacks on it were symbolic. Roman tolerance would only stretch so far.

It is irrelevant that the Greeks were taunting the Jews by setting up altars to the imperial cult; the Jews in the area were in effect stopping non-Jews sacrificing to Rome. Whether the destruction of the altar was intended as an act of defiance to Rome or not we will never know, but it could easily be construed as one. Gaius saw possible trouble and acted. Against the backdrop of the recent Alexandrian unrest, and even the Jewish resistance to Pontius Pilate's carrying of standards through Jerusalem and the putting up of golden shields on Herod's palace, Gaius decided to act promptly and in strength. For whatever reason, possibly Gaius' inexperience, Gaius could have ordered this rather apt yet rash punishment, which Philo contrasts to the supposed tolerance shown by Augustus and Tiberius.

Petronius' exact actions are a little confused due to the contradictory sources, but he probably did know trouble was brewing. He has been exalted by the sources and made a hero. Perhaps we should even doubt that he wrote to Gaius at all, and it is possible that, if he did, Gaius' order of suicide could well have been fabricated to show that God's aid was forthcoming to a man who helped the Jews.

Regardless of where and when Petronius moved, he seems to have moved troops in and encountered demonstrations. There is even evidence of armed resistance and possible revolt. Josephus (*B.J.* 2.202) sees Petronius telling Gaius that the only way they could continue would be 'to destroy the country as well as its inhabitants'. In *A.J.* 18.302, Josephus claims Gaius 'wrongly concluded that the Jews were bent on revolt'. This phrase presupposes that some would feel the Jews were doing exactly that. In *A.J.* 18.271 the Jews say 'on no account would we fight', but Josephus follows this with 'we will sooner die than violate our laws'. The *Legatio* has Petronius worrying about Jewish resistance; in 225–7 we are told that Jews came from all over to Phoenicia, 'where Petronius happened to be'; in 249 Petronius told Gaius the Jews 'might lay waste the arable land or set fire to the corn lands on the hills and the plain. He needed a guard to insure more vigilance in gathering the fruits.' It is unlikely that demonstrations on such a scale could have been completely passive. Whether or not Petronius did voice these concerns to Gaius, Philo, being a contemporary, is showing an understanding of the 'hypothetical' problems that could occur if the Jews so wanted to fight. Perhaps more telling is Tacitus' mention of the event (*Hist.* 5.9): 'then, when Gaius ordered the Jews to set up his statue in their temple, they chose rather to resort to arms'.

Behind the Jewish literary tradition of divine intervention, the sources both agree that Agrippa persuaded Gaius to change his mind. Josephus has this occurring due to a favour granted at a large dinner; Philo puts it down to friendship alone. Agrippa had plenty of reasons to intervene (beyond his love for his Jewish homeland): it was Agrippa's territory where the whole problem was taking place. A strike by the farmers would have led to hunger for his people, and this in turn to a revolt, banditry and inability to collect taxes.

Whether it was Agrippa or Petronius or any other adviser who showed Gaius the danger, or whether he even realised it himself, he decided to cancel the order for the statue. The demand for the statue would not foster loyalty to Rome; it would simply inflame an already delicate situation. Philo's concoction of Gaius' real intention in the form of a second, even bigger, statue should probably be discounted; it is perhaps simply artistic licence in order to fulfil the parameters of a divinely driven world.

Although some believe that Gaius was so convinced of his own divinity that he ordered the statue, these explanations are simplistic and merely agree with the hostile tradition. Even though we have seen reasons other than personal insult for the punishment by Gaius there is still a chance that the young and impetuous emperor was vain and that this clouded his judgement. As apt as the punishment may be, it was a little rash and bound to excite the Jews. However, there is another possibility missed by modern scholarship.

Although we can never prove what order Gaius gave, there is a chance the order was never given at all. Seneca, Suetonius and Dio are all silent on the subject, and the missing palinode casts doubt on the credibility of the whole of Philo's *Legatio* as we do not know its conclusion. The word 'palinode' that Philo uses could suggest that it is a retraction of what he has just written! Josephus would have got his information on the subject from, amongst others, Philo; similarly Tacitus would have seen the Jewish sources which mention such a command. Surely Suetonius and

Dio – the two sources that really speak of Gaius' divinity the most
– would have used such an order as ample example of his divine
aspirations. Why would they have left such a gem out of their
writings? And why would the hostile Seneca have said nothing of
it? Although the Jews were not seen as important by the Roman
authors, surely such an example of Gaius' 'madness' would be
seized! Could it be they doubted the truth of the Jewish sources?

We know that during the unrest in Alexandria the Greeks
raised statues to the imperial cult in the synagogues, perhaps
claiming to be carrying out imperial commands; the Jews would
obviously have tried to stop this, as in Jamnia where they tore
down an altar to the imperial cult. It was when in Rome that
Philo found out about the order for the statue. How did he find
out? It is doubtful he heard it from Gaius' mouth; he even tells us
a kinsman told him. It was specifically in retaliation to the tearing
down of an altar to the imperial cult that Gaius gave the command. Is it not possible that Gaius, known for his sharp wit, joked
that he would build a mighty statue of himself in the holiest place
of the Jews for their insolence? Perhaps he even threatened such
action, or discussed it without actually giving the command.
Rumours could easily spread from such a sharp tongue. The
rumour could even have been started by the Greeks themselves
among the Jews of the Diaspora to cause trouble by claiming they
were carrying out imperial instructions when defacing synagogues
with statues to the imperial cult. The whole tradition of Gaius'
personal statue in the temple could easily have come from here.
Once the Jews of the area heard such a thing, they would naturally
have demonstrated and gone on strike, or petitioned the governor
to ask if it was true. Antiochus IV had set a precedent for such a
thing by setting up his altars in the synagogues, and Pompey had
even entered the Jerusalem temple.

This hypothesis might explain why Petronius' troop movements are so confused; he merely went to the demonstrating Jews
to explain the false rumour, taking an army with him due to the
size of the force of paranoid Jews. He was reacting to a near-revolt
by the Jews. This would explain why no statue was ever built.
Similarly, it explains Petronius' survival: is it really likely he
would have gone against the word of his emperor for the sake of
the Jews? Would he really have written to Gaius asking him to

change his mind? And it might explain not only the absence from all the other sources of such a tale but also the contradictions in Josephus and Philo. The Greeks were setting up Gaius' statue in synagogues anyway; a rumour claiming Gaius was going to set one up himself in the temple could easily have spread in such a situation. It is perhaps noteworthy that Claudius' letter to the Alexandrians makes no mention of the statue issue. It would clearly be in the interests of the sources to accept and exaggerate such a rumour, therefore turning it into the historical tradition.

There is no persuasive evidence that Gaius' policy in Judaea was the result of madness. A self-confessed god would not have feared the revolt of the Jews. We cannot assume Gaius really did hate the Jews; there is not enough evidence in his actions, only in the opinions of Philo and Josephus and Gaius' supposed plans. It is the actions and events that we must study, not hearsay. And the events surrounding Gaius' treatment of the Jews show an emperor prepared to recall weak governors, but equally prepared to use legions to quash provincial trouble; two legions were enough to scare the Jews to the extent that their royal house in the guise of Agrippa got involved.

Events show that regardless of emperor there was trouble in the area. Even before Judaea was a province trouble had occurred due to inconsiderate gentile actions: around 8 BC, when Herod was nearing his demise, the Jews of Jerusalem revolted in objection to the raising of a golden eagle above the temple. It took Varus and two legions to suppress it, and afterwards Archelaus was made ethnarch – the Jews had lost their kingship. Augustus made Judaea a Roman province in AD 6 and with it showed tolerance to the Jews; standards with the emperor's face on were left at Caesarea when troops were on campaign in Judaea. Similarly, Tiberius honoured Jewish traditions by agreeing to the removal of the golden shields from the royal castle in Jerusalem.

Once Roman rule was established it was not so much the policy of individual emperors but the activities of corrupt governors that increased the problems of an area already overflowing with tensions and animosities. After all, Judaea was not all that important to the Empire. Under Tiberius, Pontius Pilate showed incompetence, ignorance and corruption; it was he who raised the shields above the royal castle, and he took the army standards through

Jerusalem. He even used money from the temple to build public amenities. It took the slaughter of Samaritans on his trip for treasure on Gerizim's holy mountain to get him recalled by Tiberius.

We have already seen Flaccus' behaviour in Alexandria, and his taking of sides against the Jews (however exaggeratedly the sources present it to us). After Gaius there were riots in Jerusalem under Ventidius Camenus, who could not control them. Ventidius' successor Felix (AD 52–60) saw urban terrorism in the same city, and under Gessius Florus (AD 64–6) the issue of Caesarea (whether it was a Jewish or Greek city) came up again, leading to riots by the Jews. Both Josephus and Tacitus accuse the procurators of Judaea of incompetence. Their ignorance and tactlessness are certain.

So, if procurators showed their ignorance of Jewish custom and handled the area badly, can we say the same of the emperors? For all the Romans' tolerance of Jewish tradition they would be confused by the monotheism of the Jews. Tiberius drew no attention to his own godhead, and it is unlikely he would have cared about local Jewish proselytism. However, he did see Judaea as a province and the Jews as subjects, and treated them so; he even deported the Jews from Rome to fight in Sardinia. We also know he expelled Jews from Rome. Perhaps Gaius' supposed hatred of the Jews had precedent elsewhere? Furthermore, Claudius expelled the Jews from Rome in AD 49, and, although he supported the civil rights of Jews in Alexandria, he could not tolerate their proselytism as he strove to maintain the stability of the Empire. There was continuous unrest in Palestine under Claudius too.

It is simplistic to say that Augustus and Tiberius tolerated the Jews whereas Gaius turned against them. Not only must we try to differentiate between the Jews of Alexandria and those of Judaea in dealing with the sources' accounts, but we have seen that, over time, the governors found Judaea a difficult province to control. There were deep-seated hatreds inherent in the area; Jews and gentiles were constantly fighting and appealing to Rome for help. Misadministration and ignorance on the part of procurators was not the fault of the emperor; when such action was made known to the emperors they acted appropriately.

If Philo's embassy had been to ask for more rights, Claudius had to answer for Gaius. And the answer was 'no'; Claudius begged tolerance towards the Greeks while confirming their current rights.

In fact, Gaius' bestowal of Judaea on Agrippa could be seen as beginning a short period of relative calm in the area. Yet again his upbringing in Rome influenced his principate; Herod Agrippa was but one loyal friend to be given territories and to serve well. Once Flaccus had been recalled, and the Jews had their short revenge on the Greeks of Alexandria, there was relative calm in Judaea under the Jewish king. Unfortunately Agrippa's death in AD 44 again gave rise to a series of procurators, which led to trouble, fighting, and, by taking away an influential protector of the Jews, the revolt of AD 66. Gaius' policy of a friendly client king had actually aided the Jews; the following procurators did not treat the orthodox faction with the respect Agrippa showed them.

Either by design or coincidence Gaius stopped the events in Alexandria by recalling Flaccus. If we trust the stories of Gaius' order for the statue, he then showed an understanding of the problem and a willingness to go back on his orders. There is not the factual evidence to back up harsh criticism of Gaius' dealings with the Jews. The revolt of AD 66 would have occurred with or without Gaius' brief reign, and his acts show a continuation of his predecessors' policy of 'tolerance' to the Jews.

## DISCUSSION

Gaius came to power to find parts of the Empire in disarray. The German border was weak; Parthia was attempting to invade Armenia and there was unrest in Alexandria. The inexperienced young emperor had to deal with all these issues, and did so forcefully. Where he decided to sort out an area with a military presence, as on the Rhine, he used strong, swift measures to deal with the situation. Where he advocated a peaceful solution, as in Armenia, he was willing to grant concessions to achieve it. Gaius showed tremendous versatility and adaptability in his foreign policy; he was willing to change the status quo for the good of the Empire, or take harsh measures in dealing with incursions. By avoiding war with Parthia, and handing the affairs of certain areas over to truly loyal client kings bound to him by friendship, he left himself free to pursue his more aggressive policies in the North. As part of a grand strategy this made perfect sense. His relations with the client kings were impeccable: Agrippa told Gaius of the stockpiling of arms by Herod, and Gaius, investigating this and finding it to be true, deposed Herod, putting his territories in the more trustworthy hands of Agrippa.

Although Gaius' reign has been seen as a hiccup in the process of the reduction of such client kings (they would be phased out by the end of the century) that is not to say they did not work. They saved on administration while ensuring loyalty – if the kings were well chosen as, indeed, Gaius' appointments were. Gaius had no problems from his client kings; he could trust men like Agrippa, Antiochus IV of Commagene and the three Thracian princes, and Rome lost nothing by surrendering Pontus, Armenia Minor and Commagene to them.

The only major provinces that Augustus and Tiberius actually incorporated were Galatia, Cappadocia and Commagene. As with Armenia, it was Claudius' annexation of Thrace that caused trouble, not Gaius' dealings with the area. Although blame could be put on Gaius for Aedemon's revolt in Mauretania, we must blame Claudius for the Thracian trouble. Tiberius' sending of Rufus to Thrace had caused trouble in AD 21 and 26; Gaius instead kept the peace while maintaining influence. Similarly, Gaius adopted a friendly policy to Aretas, king of Arabia Petraea. Gaius' only incorporation was for military necessity and, after a very short revolt, entirely successful. Gaius' preference for client kings was in fact a perfectly sound way of ensuring Roman influence over a wide area without the use of legions.

Gaius' interests lay outside Italy; he pleased the provinces with his presence, fostering loyalty. His reorganisation of Mauretania was kept, as were many of his client-king appointments – testimony to their competence. Similarly, Gaius' adding of Cilicia to Commagene remained in place. It could also have been Gaius who reorganised certain military districts of provinces such as the alpine district of Raetia; under Tiberius it had a military prefect, after Gaius it was joined with Alpes Penninae.[15] In Achaea and Macedonia – imperial provinces – Gaius maintained the status quo; early in his reign we even have evidence of Gaius showing decorum with regard to excessive numbers of statues being set up to him (*I.L.S.* 8792). This hardly backs up Gaius' supposed belief in his divinity or desire to enforce the erection of statues anywhere.

Philo, Josephus and Seneca all make out that the provinces were in a bad state of affairs on Gaius' death. The reality was that Mauretania had a small revolt – teething problems for a necessary incorporation to maintain the security of the Empire that were quickly dealt with – and the Jews were attacking the Greeks in localised trouble in Alexandria. That this latter urban unrest would not have occurred without Gaius is unlikely. The view that Gaius used the provinces for revenue does not follow the facts; the payouts to Antiochus IV and Agrippa, and the generous gifts to the three Thracian princes, contradict this.

In Gaius' foreign policy there is not much that could be described as the acts of a madman; Gaius was a competent and sensible ruler of the Empire, protecting Rome's interests with the minimum fuss and loss of life. Yet again we see a policy abroad, as with his domestic one, that would have angered the senate. Gaius not only took more power away from them with their last legion in the province of Africa but also was not scared to break Roman tradition in order to secure peace. The coming to terms with the old enemy Parthia would seem scandalous to some in the senate, and the emergence of the old client-king system would have been unpopular as it meant fewer provincial governors would be needed. As policies, these were perfectly sound; Gaius' willingness to go against the accepted status quo meant his foreign policy was adaptable and successful. His actions in the East provided the opportunity to push north and, had Gaius survived a few more years, Claudius' victories against the Chatti in AD 41 and in Britain in AD 43 would surely have been his.

Yet again, perhaps Gaius' innovations and proactive foreign policy came from a desire to prove himself both diplomatically and in the field. He had the family name Germanicus to live up to, and this would have influenced his decision to move north. Similarly, he took advantage of Germanicus' popularity in the East to pursue a peaceful policy with Parthia. And yet again, this only served to frustrate a senate who saw their frontiers shift from the East to an ambitious design on that strange island across the sea. Gaius did not change the foreign policy with the arbitrary will of a madman; he was perfectly prepared to maintain the status quo in places such as Achaea and Macedonia. His actions make sense as part of a grand strategy, and his dealings abroad were an enormous success. This caused even more bitterness amongst a senate which sat by watching the young man's popularity rise as their power was taken away from them bit by bit.

In conclusion, Gaius' short reign saw a successful foreign policy that laid the foundation for Claudius' victories. However, this policy would not have been popular with the senate, and herein lay its faults.

# 5

# CONSPIRACIES AND ASSASSINATION

Two years into Gaius' reign the *maiestas* trials returned to haunt Rome, although 'trials' is perhaps misleading. A formal charge of *maiestas* could take a long time to go through the courts, and so more often than not a quick hearing in the senate, or even *in camera*, would take place if the charge was thought to be serious (i.e. when dealing with conspirators in a plot). The sources depict Gaius as a cruel ruler, killing arbitrarily in order to pursue a reign of terror. There are countless general comments in both Suetonius and Dio claiming hundreds were killed here or there for the most trivial of reasons. Despite the sources' best efforts to depict Gaius' executions as for his own amusement or to fill the imperial coffers, when we look at the named individuals who suffered under Gaius we get a very different picture. More often than not they were involved in plots against their emperor. Dio (D.C. 59.181) writes that Gaius 'fell to plotting against many more persons than ever because of their property'; Suetonius (*Calig.* 38), Josephus (*A.J.* 19.3) and Philo (*Leg.* 105) all agree. We have already dismissed the theory that Gaius was a bankrupt, impoverishing the state by his extravagance. Now the reasons for the deaths of individuals must be looked into. After all, Gaius' reduction of the fee for informers, from a quarter to an eighth of the convicted man's property, does not tie in with the theory that he encouraged false accusations.

The twenty-five named victims in the sources seem like a high strike rate, and this requires further investigation. Most of them were in AD 39–40, and in order to strengthen the regime of Gaius. On his accession Gemellus, Silanus (his father-in-law) and the praetorian prefect Macro, with his wife, were all executed. This combination of a powerful senator, the head of the praetorian guard, and the joint heir to the throne has tempted many to speculate about a possible conspiracy. Regardless, the death of Gaius' joint heir (a boy who had a genuine blood link to Tiberius) removed a possible contender to whom dissatisfied opponents of Gaius could rally. Similar cases can be found with the deaths of Agrippa Postumus at the start of Tiberius' reign, or the death of Britannicus at the hands of Nero; such dynastic intrigue is an integral part of any hereditary succession throughout history. As for Macro, Gaius had seen the rise of Sejanus – the previous head of the praetorian guard – and its danger to Tiberius. Gaius owed the smooth running of his own accession to Macro and it is no coincidence that after his death Caligula instated a second praetorian prefect so as not to allow one man so much power. He would not make the same mistake that Tiberius made.

In AD 39 the *maiestas* trials returned in earnest. Was this really to fill the coffers of Gaius' purse, or to satiate his own bloodlust? The hostile sources try to explain the deaths in this way, so when they actually admit to conspiracies these must have been so well known in their time that they could not be passed off as the random killings of a supposedly insane tyrant. Suetonius mentions the conspiracy of Gaetulicus, Lepidus and Gaius' sisters, although it is noteworthy that he only directly alludes to the conspiracy of 'Lepidus and Gaetulicus' in his *Life of Claudius* and not in his *Life of Gaius*, which must have been done to belittle the seriousness of the affair. And, given Gaetulicus' position as commander on the Rhine, and Lepidus' marriage to Drusilla and therefore links to the imperial house, it is serious. As we have seen, Gaius marched north, arrested the conspirators, and restructured the Rhine frontier.

Dio gives a list of senatorial conspirators who were tortured and/or killed for information about plots, such as Sextus Papinius and Betilienus Bassus. A Titus Rufus supposedly stated that the 'senate thought one way and voted another' (D.C. 59.18.5); he then committed suicide, surely on the insistence of the senate itself. He was openly calling them to rally against Gaius! But those who were, were doing so in secret.

Calvisius Sabinus, legate of Pannonia, and his wife were charged on their return to Rome; he had already been prosecuted for treason in AD 32. This is an example of a senator in a position of power, with legions to hand, and a history of treason; they committed suicide before their trial. Flaccus, as we have seen, was recalled from Alexandria; we are told he was a partisan of Gemellus – further evidence that Gemellus was dangerous. He feared for his life after the death of his friend Macro; Flaccus was clearly friends with the enemies of Gaius. Interestingly, it was another conspirator, Lepidus, who pushed for his exile to a more comfortable island. Perhaps Flaccus fell foul of a clear-out of the friends of Macro, in the same way that Tiberius had attempted to get rid of the allies of Sejanus after his fall. There was one friend of Sejanus that Tiberius did not manage to rid himself of – Gaetulicus!

Despite the talk of Gaius' reign of terror and the massacre of innocents, the named victims simply do not back this up. Once plots had been uncovered there would naturally be more treason trials as unscrupulous informers sought to gain from the demise of others, exploiting the insecurity of the emperor. Similarly, the friends of the accused would be in danger. Tiberius' reign also saw suspicion and paranoia that led to executions and suicides, such as that of Vitia for allegedly lamenting the death of her son or of Mamercus Aemilius Scaurus, supposedly for writing a work of tragedy that was not to Macro's tastes. The list continues. As the tradition of treason trials is absent from Seneca and Philo, and more apparent in Suetonius and Dio, it is likely these later sources have retrojected the events of later principates, such as that of Domitian, and have mapped them on to their history of not only Gaius but also Tiberius, which would explain these clear exaggerations.

Gaius' victims, on the whole, were privy to, or involved in, conspiracies against him. There were serious plots against Gaius throughout his reign. An Anicius Cerealis, who committed suicide in AD 66 under Nero, was 'hated' because he betrayed a conspiracy against Gaius (Tac. *Ann.* 15.74/16.17). We also have examples of those who were tortured but did not divulge any information, such as the actress Quintilia and Lucius Junior. Many of those who fell during the reign of Gaius were of senatorial rank; it would not be long before a conspiracy was successful.

In late January, AD 41, Caligula was assassinated while leaving the theatre by Chaerea and a host of assassins. Seneca tells us Chaerea and Asiaticus Valerius had the main parts. Josephus gives the most detailed account (*A.J.* 19), whereby three plots were being hatched by Aemilius Regulus, Cassius Chaerea, the head of the praetorian guard, and Annius Vinicianus. Regulus supposedly hated unjust proceedings; Vinicianus wanted revenge for Lepidus, and Chaerea wanted to prove his manliness. All wanted to preserve the city and the Empire. The praetorian prefect M. Arrecinus Clemens was involved, as were Papinius and Sabinus, both military tribunes. The conspirators were not all senators, but the aftermath of the assassination clearly shows their aim: a meeting of the senate was convened on the Capitol where Gnaeus Sentius Saturninus made a speech advocating restoration of the Republic. The final plot, conceived by high-standing senators, sought to overthrow the principate altogether. Chaerea and Sabinus have been seen as instruments of the senatorial plotters, and it seems there were many senators involved: Vatinius, Cluvius Rufus, P. Nonius Asprenas, Vinicianus and Saturninus. In short, the senate brought about the demise of Gaius. It was more than likely that both Chaerea and Clemens had either Republican beliefs or personal grudges. Despite there being no need for a praetorian guard under a Republic, these assassins would be instrumental in the creation of a new Republic; they were experienced soldiers and there would always be posts for such men in the army or in the provinces. The leaders of the conspiracy would reward these hired assassins; it is unlikely they would find themselves out of work after the death of Caligula if there was a return to the Republic!

We have seen the unpopularity of Gaius with the senate, or part of it, but is there evidence for discontent amongst other strata of Roman society? Again the sources generalise and do their best to portray Gaius as unpopular across the board. Josephus writes: 'there was no one who would not have reckoned the removal of Gaius as a blessing' (*A.J.* 19.62). So we are led to believe everyone backed his assassination; we will soon see how inaccurate this is. Suetonius and Dio fill their works with anecdotes describing Gaius' mistreatment of his people; Suetonius states that Gaius would sometimes 'shut up the granaries and condemn the people to hunger' (*Calig.* 26). Dio has Gaius mixing in pieces of iron with the coins he threw to the people at his *congiaria*, 'and many perished in their efforts to grab it' (59.25.5). He even has Gaius massacre civilians in the Circus! Had a contemporary told such a tale it might have had a larger chance of being truth, but Dio, just under two hundred years later, is surely exaggerating. The people would have hated such a man as the sources portray. And the lack of such a tale in Seneca or any other contemporary speaks volumes. As for the soldiers, Gaius' supposed attempt to massacre the two legions that revolted in Germany on Tiberius' death would not have endeared him to them.

The acts surrounding Gaius' death, however, do not back up such discontent in the people and soldiers of Rome. Josephus talks of the 'no small danger that menaced the emperor's assassins' once the deed was done (*A.J.* 19.119). Why would there be any danger if everyone agreed with his murder? Gaius' German bodyguard was first on the scene and began a virtual riot, attempting to find the senatorial killers. Of course, Josephus attributes their vengeance not to loyalty or love for their emperor but to the gifts of money he gave them; if he was dead, their actions would not gain them any more gifts and they were not to know the attitude of Gaius' successor towards them. They killed Asprenas, Norbanus and Anteius – all senators. Josephus tells us they acted only for their own advantage. This killing spree would not help them as Gaius was already dead. They had nothing to gain from searching out Gaius' killers; their actions show their obvious sorrow at his death.

Similarly, the army and the praetorian guard had no desire for the death of Gaius or a return to the Republic. Josephus' description of the news reaching the theatre is important. Those who were happy at his death supposedly remained silent out of fear; 'there were others to whom the news was quite contrary to their hopes because they had no desire that any such thing should befall Gaius . . . among them were silly women, children, all the slaves, and some of the army' (J. *A.J.* 19.128–9). So the groups that were not ambitious for power did not want Gaius dead. Had his rule been detrimental to their society in any way (say, in the economy or their public freedoms) then they would have rejoiced in his death. Josephus feels the need to explain why; that is, he defends the conspirators and sees the most part of the population – a people evidently very happy with Gaius – as 'silly'. Tiberius' end was greeted with rapturous applause – not so that of Caligula.

Josephus sees the army as 'partners in his tyranny'; the women and youth were 'captivated by his shows' and enjoyed free meat distributions. Naturally, Josephus has such benevolence as down to Gaius' own savagery! Finally, the slaves supported Gaius as they found refuge in him from their masters and could gain wealth by informing. (We have already seen that Gaius took measures to stop informers.)

In fact, Gaius' enemies are seen as purely 'patricians' (J. *A.J.* 19.132). That Josephus talks of the plotters feeling fear clearly shows that they were well aware people would mourn the loss of Gaius and seek vengeance; the German bodyguard did exactly that. We are told that the populace searched for Gaius' killers, whereas the senate only made pretence of doing so. The consuls actually had to put forth a decree that forced the people and soldiers to go home, promising the soldiers money if they refrained from rioting. The senators wanted the people and soldiers to retire as they did not support the senate's cause; they were perfectly satisfied with Gaius. The praetorians wanted a new emperor and chose Gaius' uncle, Claudius. The fact that the army clearly resented Gaius' death puts into serious doubt the inane stories of Gaius' military exploits, as given by Suetonius and Dio (i.e. the forcing of soldiers to pick up shells; the attempted massacre of two legions; running away at the first sight of the enemy on the Rhine). Such a man would not have endeared himself to the soldiers.

The fact that the plotters held arms shows they feared that Gaius' supporters would seek vengeance or try to stop them. When Josephus talks of the stand-off between Claudius and the senate he states that the senate had four cohorts on its side (*A.J.* 19.188; in *B.J.* 2.205 they have only three). He even says: 'by this time the people were also withdrawing, overjoyed and full of hope and pride because they had acquired self-government and no longer were under a master. Chaerea was everything to them'

(J. *A.J.* 19.189). Yet Claudius had to bow to public opinion and have him killed; Chaerea clearly was not that popular with the people. Josephus feels that once he has explained the reasons behind the various factions' love for Gaius, he can then ignore it and simply say they were happy 'by this time'. This is clearly unlikely. The people probably loved the man who had 'no strength to resist the flatteries of the mob' (J. *A.J.* 19.202).

The praetorians 'raged throughout the palace in their fury' (J. *A.J.* 19.214), but supposedly felt Gaius had justly met his fate. They were determined to have Claudius as emperor; had Gaius been so unpopular they would not have turned to Claudius. Josephus has Germanicus' good reputation enforcing Claudius as candidate; if Gaius had been so bad, this name would surely have been blackened and the populace would not have wanted to make the same mistake twice. Having told us that the people withdrew, happy that they no longer had a master, Josephus goes on to explain that the 'will of the people and that of the senators were at variance' (*A.J.* 19.227). In other words, only the conspiratorial senators wanted Gaius dead and a return to the Republic. The sources say that Gaius detested the equestrian order; Suetonius even gives a plan of Gaius' that involved massacring the noblest senators and equestrians and then moving the capital to Alexandria! Gaius actually seems to have taken an interest in the upkeep of the order; he revised their lists, brought in new men and let them perform on the stage. (Claudius' attempts to shame them shows their willingness to perform.)

There is no serious evidence of discontent with Gaius in any section of Roman society other than the senatorial order. After Julius Caesar's death there had been riots when the senate banned the dictatorship; the people had been happy with Julius as they were with Gaius. Even with the anecdotes, such as the imperial brothel, Dio explains: 'the multitude, however, was not greatly displeased with the proceedings, but actually rejoiced with him in his licentiousness' (59.28.10).

There is, therefore, evidence for unpopularity only with the senate: senators conspired against Gaius, and when they succeeded were unpopular for killing the emperor; Claudius had to bow to public opinion and execute Chaerea and Lupus, the senators' assassins, for their part in the plot. The 'victims' of the *maiestas* trials were not simply victims of economics or cruelty – Gaius was probably no more cruel than his peers. Gaius' policy at home and abroad was sound. The break with the senate did not come about because Gaius was cruel or insane. The question remains, therefore, why Gaius was killed at all; how did the senate fall out with Gaius?

# 6

## GAIUS AND THE SENATE

One of the most important factors in the problem of the reign of Gaius is timing. Gaius, like Tiberius, inherited Augustus' legacy – an impossible system of *princeps* and senate. The *princeps* had, de facto, ultimate power. The senate had been used to ruling Rome and only since AD 14 had they had to contend with an emperor who instantly inherited his position as leader of the Romans, including the senate. In the Republic, senators strove to gain *auctoritas*, and with it came political power. A hereditary succession destroyed this system. Although Augustus ruled via his *auctoritas*, and the transition to Tiberius was smooth as the latter already possessed political clout and a reputation, when Gaius inherited the Empire he took all the powers of his predecessors without having any *auctoritas* whatsoever. The system was new and in its early stages. To Gaius, the senate was imposed on him, and was not a personal, hand-picked council. As a body it felt it was too important just to be a committee, but it was not powerful enough to impose its will. It was full of aristocratic nobles of famous lineage whose ancestors had served Rome and earned their place in history. These men had the family background and the ability to serve Rome well. Augustus set up his principate slowly and Tiberius was his first successor.

Tiberius' way of dealing with the senate was to give them as much authority as he could, while ensuring his manipulation.

He had been, after all, a senator himself. Ultimately, he failed in his relationship with them and his reign fell into the bloodshed of the *maiestas* trials. Certain senators resented the emperor, but as a body the senate did not want to go against a man with ultimate power; their fear and uncertainty meant they were incapable of independent action.[1] They had become dependent upon the *princeps* for their own careers.

Tiberius had been a dedicated attendee of senatorial meetings while he was in Rome; he consulted the senate, even if they were rapidly becoming a rubber stamp for his policies. At least their continued involvement – that is, in voting honours and controlling legislative, religious, diplomatic and judicial functions – kept the orders busy; sessions were both frequent and time-consuming. The senate was respected, honoured and involved throughout the first years of Tiberius' reign; he even took the elections from the *comitia* and handed them to the senate in order to save them the bother of canvassing. Unfortunately, once Tiberius left for Capreae, the whole system turned more and more into an autocracy, with the senate referring matters continually to the emperor as they feared going against his wishes. The retirement of Tiberius highlighted the massive problems of the Augustan system. Once the treason trials had kicked in things got worse. As a senator, if you were not with the emperor (or Sejanus) you were against him. Tiberius had tried to involve the senate, but soon fell out with the obsequious body.

Gaius – only the second unfortunate inheritor of the Augustan system – gave the senate a new start, or so they hoped. His accession put an end to the treason trials and gave a clean break to a much depleted senate; the senate instantly voted this son of Germanicus practically all the powers of his predecessors in one go. They did not expect him to use them. Gaius had not been a senator; he had been present with Tiberius on Capreae from AD 31 to witness the height of the *maiestas* trials, the dominance of Sejanus and the rift between emperor and senate. Furthermore, he had no memory of the Republic or its workings; he had grown up under the principate. He had no aspirations of sharing power with a body surplus to requirements; he had no need for the senate. He saw no shame in letting his foreign friends run the provinces for him by reverting back to the client-king system. To obtain a political position it was more important to be a friend of the emperor than it was to be a senator. For example, the always overlooked Claudius was chosen to be a consul with Gaius. He may have been a senator, but his ties to Gaius were of much greater importance. The senate may have been the class from which Gaius drew officials, but their *auctoritas* or senatorial status was not important; their friendship to Gaius was. Lepidus was honoured more for his family ties to Gaius via his marriage to Gaius' sister than his ability to govern, his *auctoritas* or his senatorial status. Gaius' encouragement of provincials and equestrians to join the senate further undermined the importance of the senatorial rank or having respect within that body. It was becoming simply a pool from which to draw officials, and to which Gaius' friends could be added and from which his enemies expelled. Claudius would continue this treatment of the senate, this disregard for the order, but with a lot more discretion. Gaius' view of the principate was completely new; it was his empire and he would act as the emperor. By contrast, the senate saw Tiberius' death and the accession of a young and inexperienced emperor as a chance to flex their muscles once again.

Gaius held four consulships during his reign, showing his intention to be directly involved in the governing of the Empire. He wanted to dominate the order. The mechanisms of that empire meant Gaius had to go through the senate, even if he saw that body as surplus to requirements. His number of consulships shows his desire to dominate the senatorial proceedings. He disregarded the rank of its members, while trying to pull power away from the body. He also maintained a high profile in the city and with the army on the battlefield. Alston sees his lack of rank, experience and honours as forcing him to involve himself in order to increase his *auctoritas*.[2] This is true, but it would also seem he set out to rule directly. He certainly made sure he was at the heart of government. He could not rely on reputation, as his predecessors both could; he had not been a senator, and was not respected for past deeds. So he had to choose a different path from Tiberius' tactic of distant manipulation of the senate. To a certain extent, Gaius was forced into involvement. And this involvement could only be unpopular with the senate.

It is possible that Gaius' nervousness about a body composed of men not only much more distinguished than he was for their exploits, but also much older and wiser than himself, led him to certain acts. There is a distinct policy of removing power from the hands of the senate: he deprived individual senators of their last chance of commanding a legion in their own right, with their own *imperium*; he returned the elections to the people; he even told them how to vote. He did not keep up the Augustan pretence that the senate was important and involved in the decision-making process. To Gaius the senate was simply a mechanism for legislation; it was of no real value to him. However, he was fully aware that he could not completely do away with it. He understood the workings of the principate and sought to dominate this mechanism of government. This, coupled with his lack of respect for senators (i.e. forcing them to put on shows, allowing them to perform, dismissing the suffect consuls of AD 39), alienated the senatorial class. There was no detrimental effect on Roman society or policy; the common people could well have despised the senatorial rank anyway. Nero was certainly popular for humiliating the upper classes. However, there would be a detrimental effect for Gaius. As a newcomer, he required the support of the senate and the army for his whole political position. Although Gaius involved himself with the latter, personally going on campaign, his refusal to respect and involve the senate undermined his attempts to reform the principate radically.

Gaius' reign, therefore, was a direct contrast to that of Tiberius; there was no façade of friendship or respect for the senate. Furthermore, Rome became a virtual carnival with shows of every kind; Gaius seemed to be following the imaginary advice of Maecenas to Augustus to adorn the capital with utter disregard of expense and make it magnificent with festivals of every kind. The senate saw Gaius' popularity soar with his lavish entertainments policy, while they had their powers curtailed and were forced to please the masses at their own expense. To some, it was the mark of a tyrant to court popularity with the *plebs*. As the senate of old was becoming defunct, Gaius was too popular with the masses; certainly they would not have had any sympathy with their upperclass countrymen. Although the senate was aware of its faltering power under Tiberius' last years, his death gave them new hopes – new hopes dashed by Gaius very quickly indeed. Gaius' view of the principate did not require them as individuals. The rank of senator had become a sham, dependent entirely upon the will of the emperor. Whereas Augustus made an issue of being *princeps* over emperor – first citizen over king – Gaius set about creating a role for the emperor himself, taking power from the senate in the process. He was the first emperor to have spent his whole life under the principate, and was a clear product of it.

Augustus had packed the senate with his supporters to ensure its co-operation. Tiberius, having been a senator for so long, and having friends in the senate, found an already compliant senate on his accession – a senate with members who personally knew him and were on good terms with him, such as Marcus Lepidus and Gnaeus Piso. It took years for them to turn against him. Gaius, however, was not shrewd enough to bring a sufficient number of his supporters into the senate. From the outset he simply dominated the order and gave important positions to his friends. This was a grave mistake and immediately turned them against him. Claudius learned from Gaius' mistakes; he continued his predecessor's attempts at setting up an autocracy, but with much more discretion. He honoured the senate while obtaining more power for his freedmen and so for himself. Like Augustus and Tiberius, he knew that the *princeps* and senate were not compatible unless the senate was fully co-operative. Therefore he held a censorship in the years AD 47–8 to deal with just that problem. He put new men – his men – into the order while condemning those against him; Claudius then exerted a greater personal direct control over it. By promoting provincials into the senate, he was guaranteeing their obedience to him through gratitude.

Just as in the case of Gaius, once the senate realised what was happening there were plots against him, such as that of Marcus Furius Camillus Scribonianus in AD 42 with his Dalmatian legions – but to no avail. Claudius extended his independence from the senate by putting more power in the hands of his secretariat, made up of slaves and freedmen. Claudius went further than Gaius by centralising administration to such an extent that he destroyed the independence of the *aerarium* and diminished the importance of senators in the army even further. He continued the policies of Gaius in a more extreme and yet more shrewd way, hiding behind false respect for the order. He was altogether more cautious in his dealings with the senate, and less open.

Gaius had seen Tiberius' attempts to involve the senate fail and the end of his reign spiral into *maiestas* trials and bloodshed; hence Gaius' denunciation of the senate in AD 39, fulminating against them for bringing on the *maiestas* trials themselves. Gaius tried the opposite tactic and sought to remove as much power as possible from the ancient order. Claudius had seen his predecessor's failings: Gaius was too overt in claiming power for himself. It is no surprise that Claudius learnt from Gaius and adjusted his actions, while keeping the same aim – to pull power further away from the senate, thereby setting up a stronger hereditary regime.

Gaius' success throughout the Empire – peace abroad, with prosperity and popularity at home – highlighted the impotence and pointlessness of the senatorial body. His use of client kings instead of provincial governors drawn from the senate gave the body less opportunity to advance. Had the senate not had aspirations of governing (or simply not existed), Gaius and his advisers could have ruled successfully for years and remained popular. As we have seen, his policies were sound for his empire.

# 7

## CONCLUSION

Beyond the exaggerated generalisations or anecdotes in the sources, there is no evidence that Gaius was a bad governor or unpopular with anyone other than senators. Nero and Domitian persecuted the senate and in doing so pleased the masses, and for their trouble they too were remembered as 'tyrants'. Gaius' death came about because the senate saw their decline and lost the respect of their emperor, while Gaius gained more and more popularity. His assassination was a major attempt to restore the Republic. What the senate originally saw as a chance to reassert itself over their new, young emperor by advising him soon became impossible. Gaius went beyond all senatorial expectation and took power away from them; their only chance at claiming that power back was to assassinate their master as soon as possible; a working relationship with the young ruler had proved impossible. There had been no fresh start.

The tradition of a cruel and insane tyrant came from senatorial 'historians' writing after Gaius and when Claudius had successfully implemented a campaign of denigration of his nephew. He had to show that it was Gaius who was at fault and not the principate itself. Seneca's writings are not history, and we can see in them the success that Claudius' denigration of Gaius had. Suetonius and Dio wrote when the legend of Gaius had already been formed, and used history written by Claudius and hostile senatorial sources, such as Cluvius Rufus. The religious-political writings of the Jewish sources used Gaius as a character; they were not interested in impartial history.

The timing of Gaius' reign has been understated by modern scholarship; his way of dealing with the senate and his vision for the principate were not compatible with a senate aware of its decline and hoping for a new, young ruler it could manipulate. Momigliano has pointed out that the whole Julio-Claudian line from Augustus to Nero was preoccupied with the protection of the house from the senate or a usurper.[1] This explains the paranoia necessary for the *maiestas* trials to come about. Each had to tackle the Augustan system. Gaius was the most up-front and open, hence his quick demise. He has been seen as the first undisguised master of the Roman state. No emperor, this early on in the principate, could so completely alienate the senate and survive. Gaius' lack of *auctoritas* on becoming *princeps* contrasted dramatic-ally with that of his predecessors. This in turn may have led him to close as many doors as possible to senators – he did not want individuals gaining even more prestige as it would highlight his complete lack of experience.

The named victims of Gaius' reign were not victims of Gaius' cruelty or economics, as we have seen. Once begun, the *maiestas* trials were hard to stop. In such circumstances the fear of even just being friends with an enemy of the emperor could lead to suicide. An emperor could not ban *maiestas* or informing as he would run the risk of falling foul of a real plot. In defence of Tiberius' trials and so-called reign of terror, Tacitus does not seem to support the picture painted by Suetonius and Dio. Perhaps if we had Tacitus' account of Gaius' reign we could come to similar conclusions.

By leaving the generalisations aside and focusing on the particulars of the sources (the major events, acts and named 'victims'), without Gaius' supposed plans or desires, we get a very different picture of his reign from that of the cruel madman. Modern scholarship has not gone far enough in showing Gaius for what he was: a competent, young, intelligent emperor whose death came about because he wanted to rule completely, as befits an emperor. He had a clear manifesto for ruling the Empire, which blocked any real involvement by the senate – a senate he had been taught to distrust by his time on Capreae. Exposed to his mother, obsessed by their family's right to rule, and to the popularity of his father Germanicus, Caligula would have grown up convinced of his own destiny. Unfortunately the extent of his political experience was observing Tiberius while on Capreae; it is no wonder he set out to rule directly and without the help of an unwanted senate. He was a product of the principate; his death came about not because he was a cruel incompetent whose reign saw injustice as he played 'with the resources of the Empire' (Sen. *Brev. Vit.* 18.5), but because the senate were at a crisis point in their history and so attempted to rid themselves of the principate altogether. Gaius' assassination was an attempt by the senate to restore the Republic. Its failure ensured that Gaius' work would be continued by his successors and that a new role for the emperor had been created.

# APPENDIX 1

# THE SOURCES

To undertake this study successfully the literary sources must be treated with caution, especially the personal traits and fetishes that they continually ascribe to the emperor, and we must try to strip them down to the basic events.[1] Gaius' supposed personal preoccupations shed no light on this study, which takes a more rigorously political approach, evaluating his policies and not his hobbies. We must remember that the ancient literary sources were not 'objective' in the modern sense. They each chose what events to portray, and then wrote their own interpretation of them. So certain deeds are missed out completely. In fact, silence on certain issues can speak volumes! We can exploit the various agendas of each literary source; they do not each leave out the same information and so by collating the various events of Gaius' reign from all sources we get a more comprehensive picture of the period. A source can decide to report only successes or only failings, and then exaggerate these with personal interpretation. Sources select according to their agendas; it is our job to pool all the reliable parts of each individual source. Criteria must be established for the treatment of the sources so as not to accept or reject various parts of them arbitrarily. For example, we can accept that there was a German expedition, and that both Lepidus and Gaetulicus were executed, but we should be sceptical about accepting the reasons given for these events in the sources. Suetonius tells us that the march north was undertaken on a whim as Gaius had been advised by an oracle to recruit more Batavians; Dio gives his usual economic explanation. One must draw one's own conclusions from the series of events. Therefore by avoiding the generalisations and concentrating on the particulars we will achieve a much more satisfactory picture of Gaius' reign. Similarly, the evaluative and interpretative comments must be treated with caution; we will re-evaluate Gaius' reign using the particulars of his rule – the foreign policy, the executions, the taxes. Opinions that the sources give us must be accepted only if they are backed up with evidence to prove them. After all, each of the sources has its own agenda and therefore each portrays events accordingly. It is unlikely that the sources, however biased, would concoct, say, the death of a prominent figure or the bridge at Baiae: they could, however, exaggerate the reasons for them, falsify their cause or add partisan evaluation. It is these events that lay the basis for this study and not the exaggerated reasons for them (i.e. madness). In fact, analysing Gaius' state of mind should be avoided altogether. Most sources, when ascribing insanity to him, are not comment-ing on a clinical condition. From our position, almost two thousand years later and with unreliable sources at best, it would be foolish to try to diagnose Gaius' mental health specifically. Instead we will evaluate his policies, and look for evidence of an unsound mind here. In short, we must distrust the interpretations given in the sources and concentrate on the events.

The 'philosopher' Seneca published most of his works under Claudius and Nero. His attempts to secure his recall from exile by Claudius make much of what he writes simply obsequious tracts that criticise Gaius in order to ingratiate himself with Claudius; he was following Claudius' lead of denigrating his predecessor. The fact that his later works, such as the *Apocolocyntosis*, mock Claudius in order to flatter Nero confirm this; we simply cannot trust his opinions as evidence for history. Moreover, his position as a Stoic, combined with his philosophical views, coloured his atti-tude to absolute rulers. Gaius is his continual example of an evil despot. For example, Seneca tells us that a son of Pastor was killed, but the reason given – that he was 'foppish' – must surely be distrusted (Sen. *Ira.* 2.33.3–7). He wrote philosophical tracts, not history, and so is of limited and incidental use in a discussion of Gaius' policy, though he seems to have been personally acquainted with Gaius.

Another contemporary of Gaius who wrote on the period is Philo. His treatises, *In Flaccum* and *Legatio ad Gaium*, have been seen as political propaganda. Being a Jew, his works are naturally religious, as well as political, and he shows Gaius in the light of his dealings with the Jews; this contemporary was a member of the embassy to Gaius in AD 40, and has written two tracts con-cerning the period. *In Flaccum*, published *c.* AD 38, explains the trouble in Alexandria of the same year and Flaccus' fall. The *Legatio ad Gaium*, written under Claudius, describes both the embassy to Gaius and Gaius' dealings with the Jews. A proud Jew,

Philo sees the enemies of Judaism as enemies of God. Both Flaccus and Gaius are castigated in the *In Flaccum* and the *Legatio* respectively, and divine intervention sees to their removal at key moments. This belief in divine intervention is deeply woven into Philo's literary works, and as a consequence events are manipulated. Gaius is, for example, seen as the saviour in *In Flaccum*, ending the violence in Alexandria by recalling Flaccus; in the *Legatio* he is the villain, and the violence in Alexandria ends only on his death. Similarly, Gaius is presumably prompted to arrest Flaccus by Agrippa in *In Flaccum* as he passed on the grievances of the Jews to Gaius in a 'decree'. Yet the *Legatio* shows the decree as useless – Jewish hopes rest on the embassy. In fact, far from being the saviour, Gaius is blamed for the civil unrest in Alexandria by a manipulation of chronology. Philo's works have been seen as political propaganda. After Gaius' death, the Jews needed Claudius' sympathies for reprisals against the Alexandrian Greeks. Therefore the Jews are depicted as innocent victims of unprovoked aggression. Philo has Gaius' arrest of Flaccus down to misadministration (playing down other personal motives) to set an example for future governors. The *Legatio* is full of talk about the strength and numbers of the Jews across the Empire (e.g. *Leg.* 43–52 in Macro's speech). Philo represents the Jews in the Roman Empire, and is writing invective and not history in order to get his message across. Gaius' so-called 'indescribable hatred of the Jews' (*Leg.* 133) is a clear exaggeration. Agrippa was one of Gaius' best friends, and Gaius even let the Jews have a king – something Augustus had taken away from them. This would surely have made the Greeks angry. In the *Legatio* Philo has Gaius renouncing his promise not to set up a statue at Jerusalem, by his secret planning of a second. This smacks of a corroboration simply to serve the necessary conception of divine intervention. Had Gaius agreed not to set up his image, and meant it, then God would have no need to kill him! For all this, Philo was a contemporary and so it is unlikely the events he gives us are not accurate in essence, however exaggerated. It is unlikely he made up the riot of Alexandria, but he could have left out of his work any events that portrayed the Jews in a bad light.

Another Jew, Josephus, also writes on the period and gives a lengthy account of Gaius' assassination which, because of its detail, many scholars see as based on a contemporary Roman source. Added to his obvious religious bias is the fact that Josephus was an aristocrat who saw his country and class devastated by the Jewish revolt of AD 66 – a revolt to which he was opposed. He owed to Vespasian both his life in Rome and his chance to write history, and depicts the Flavian emperors in a good light. As there was trouble in Judaea under Gaius' reign, helping to bring about the war, Josephus may have felt personal antipathy towards Gaius. Josephus, writing from the late 60s, and having published *Bellum Judaicum* by AD 79 and *Antiquitates Judaicae* by AD 93/4, was involved in the Jewish revolt of AD 66, despite disagreeing with such action. He abandoned a suicide pact with his comrades, and was taken to Rome by Vespasian; in short he owed his fortune, life and his chance to write history to the Flavian emperors. A spokesman for the Jewish faith and an aristocrat (from an aristocracy decimated by fighting the Romans), he advocated a working relationship with Rome. He claims to write the truth and criticises historians who 'collected from hearsay casual and contradictory stories which they have then edited in a rhetorical style' (*B.J.* 1, 1–2); in *A.J.* 8, 36 he states 'I have said nothing but the truth.' He has been seen as a missionary and apologist for his people. Despite his Roman connections he still exhibits Jewish traits in his literature: divine intervention is seen as the reason for Gaius' death. From a personal point of view, a man who was against a revolt would not think highly of anyone who soured Romano-Jewish relations before the conflict, and Gaius did not go out of his way to improve the relationship.

The biographer Suetonius' works are interested mainly in scandal and rumour; his main concern is with the character of his subjects and he seems even to assess emperors more by their virtues and vices than by their policies. In fact, after chapter 22 Suetonius' *Life of Gaius* simply reads as a list of atrocities. Therefore much of what Suetonius says is not illuminating to this work on Gaius' government. He is also writing in the second century with a clear idea of how a *princeps* should behave. He has a set idea of what a good emperor should be doing, and gives credit to those who protect the social hierarchies; bad treatment of distinguished families is always looked down upon. Furthermore, Suetonius' works are littered with exaggerations and contradictions. For example, he has Gaius constantly berating the equestrians for being devotees of the stage and arena, yet Gaius is supposed to have loved such shows himself. He turns everything against Gaius where he can: the boy's silence and a lack of emotion on Capreae over the deaths of his mother and brother are depicted as a fault when he could merely have been trying to save his own life! Suetonius even has Tiberius, that 'shrewd old man', trying to soften Gaius' savage nature with singing and dancing. He did have access to official records, and so he should be consulted for information on, say, policy, however much we disregard his slant on Gaius' character.

Finally, Dio is the literary source furthest away from the period, but the only proper historian. However, he wrote more than 150 years later and would have used, amongst others, the previous sources. His account is confused, especially because we have to rely on epitomes in some areas. Parts are also missing – for example, Dio breaks off at the beginning of D.C. 59.25. Like Suetonius, he is writing with a definite idea of how an emperor should govern (see his Maecenas speech to Augustus: 52.14–40). His works are full of anecdotes and vivid descriptions; this plagues his account of Gaius. His subject matter is that which would concern senators; he writes from their point of view. Unfortunately his characteristic avoidance of detail means events are often missed out completely.

Josephus, Suetonius and Dio all probably used the Roman historians of the first century. We do not know anything about their individual works, only their names – M. Servilius Nonianus, Aufidius Bassus, Fabius Rusticus and Cluvius Rufus. They were all men of high standing, if not involved in governing themselves, and so naturally adverse to Gaius' autocratic way of ruling, as we will see. Furthermore, those writing under Claudius and beyond would have followed his policy of denigrating his predecessor; as a historian himself Claudius would certainly have influenced their works and so we can assume they were anti-Caligulan in senti-ment. Unfortunately we do not have Tacitus' *Annals* for Gaius' reign, and he is much more respected as a historian. Only a few comments in his other works survive. It is perhaps telling, there-fore, that he dismisses the accounts of these men as being un-reliable because they were written under the influence of recent 'hatred' (Tac. *Ann.* 1.1). In short, sources that painted Gaius in a poor light were used by the literary sources we have at our disposal.

There are also various non-literary sources which shed some light on Gaius' reign. Coinage of the period is extremely important as it shows what the emperor wanted to depict on the coins as he chose what images were used on them. This is a clear mark of what he wanted accentuated about his reign or character, and even what he disregarded. There are various inscriptions, such as the Fasti (a calendar that gives important information) and the Arval Brethren Records (a priestly college headed by the emperor himself). Both give the dates of important events, magistracies, and help us piece together the events of Gaius' reign. There is also archaeological evidence which shows us the extent of Gaius' building programme. Because of the fact that the literary sources are tainted by the authors' bias, these other sources are all very important in trying to find out the truth about Gaius' rule, as they give us a different slant.

By bearing in mind the motives of the literary sources, and by ignoring their empty generalisations and distrusting their interpretation, we will be moving away from rumour and using Gaius' actions – for example his politics, his military campaigns – as the basis of this study. Although we must not discount rumour altogether, as it could be indicative of the reactions of certain people, we must treat the five major literary sources with circumspection in this review of the reign of the emperor Gaius. We will form our own interpretation of his rule from the reign itself, which we must carefully extract from all the sources at our disposal.

# GLOSSARY OF LATIN TERMS

**Aedile**  An administrative post and another step in the *cursus honorum*. The bearer was in charge of the administration of the city of Rome.

**Aerarium militare**  The treasury that paid out discharge bounties to veterans. It was set up in AD 6 by Augustus.

**Auctoritas**  This concept, which was central to the Augustan principate, is hard to render precisely; it means 'influence' and 'prestige', and embraces the idea of acquiring these through a combination of heredity, personality and achievement. Importantly, it implies the ability to patronise on a large scale.

**Clementia**  This means 'clemency', or being sparing to political adversaries: whilst it might on particular occasions be welcome in its effects, in principle it was a 'virtue' related to men of overwhelming (and, thus, unwelcome) power, which could be denied as capriciously as it was exercised.

**Comitia**  Popular assembly. The *Comitia centuriata* was the assembly of the Roman people which, during the Republic, elected the consuls and praetors, and could pass legislation once it had been put forward by the senate.

**Congiarium**  A distribution of gifts made by the emperor to his subjects.

**Consul**  The *consul* was the head of the executive branch of government during the Republic; two were elected each year, and were accountable to the electorate for their tenure of office. They presided over meetings of the senate and assemblies of the *populus* (whole people), and, until the late third century BC, regularly commanded the armies in battle, until this function was increasingly taken over by promagistrates (*proconsul, propraetor*). Under the principate, whilst prestige still attached to the office, its importance came to relate more to the provincial and army commands for which it represented a 'qualification'. Also under the principate it became normal for the consuls who took office on 1 January (*ordinarii*), and who gave their names to the year, to resign midway through the year in favour of replacements (*consules suffecti*). This was a method of increasing the numbers of men qualified for senior commands.

**Cursus Honorum** The ladder of office climbed during the Republic by senators in their quest for the consulship; it was subject to a number of organising laws (e.g. the *Lax Villia* of 180 BC, and a *Lex Cornelia* of Sulla), which laid down intervals between offices as well as the proper order for holding them. Under the principate, the *cursus* remained in place, though a man's progress along it was affected by imperial favour (or the lack of it), and by the number of his legitimate children. The chief offices under the principate (and ages of tenure) were:

| *Office* | *Age* |
| --- | --- |
| Vigintivirate (board of twenty) | 18 |
| Military tribune | 21–2 |
| Quaestor | 25 |
| Tribune of the plebs (often omitted) | |
| Aedile (often omitted) | |
| Praetor | 30–5 |
| Legionary commander (*legatus legionis*) | 30+ |
| Consul | 37+ |
| Proconsul or *legatus Augusti* | 38+ |

**Dies nefastus** An 'unlucky' day. *Dies nefasti* were days on which no judgement could be pronounced, nor public business transacted.

**Dignitas** This 'dignity' referred specifically to the holding of offices of the *cursus honorum*. It was, for example, an affront to Caesar to be barred from competing for a second consulship, which by 50 BC he was entitled to do. Similarly, Tiberius took it as an affront to his *dignitas* that in 6 BC he was given tribunician power simply to annoy Gaius and Lucius Caesar.

**Dominatio** The state of being a master (*dominus*): the word originally and properly referred to the state of being a master of slaves, but is increasingly used to describe the position and behaviour of Julius Caesar and (by some) of Augustus.

**Equites** Members of the equestrian order were during the principate Rome's second social class. Originally a rather disparate body, the order acquired coherence through its commercial activities following the expansion of the Empire from the second century BC. Companies formed within the order (*societates*) undertook (for profit) many tasks during the Republic of a civil service nature. Augustus reorganised the order so that it had a career structure in which it carried out similar tasks but for salaries rather than profits.

**Imperium** The executive *power* bestowed on consuls and praetors during the Republic, through which they 'controlled' the state. *Imperium* was tenable as it was defined – consular, proconsular. Augustus under the first settlement controlled Gaul, Spain and Syria under a proconsular *imperium*, which was enhanced to superiority over others (*maius*) under the second settlement. He had a permanent 'residual' *imperium*, which could be temporarily redefined to enable him to undertake other tasks, such as censorial duties.

**Latus clavus** The broad purple stripe worn on the robes of senators to symbolise rank. Augustus is said to have allowed the sons of senators to wear it in order to encourage their entry into the order.

**Legatus** Originally a man to whom 'assistant' power was delegated; Pompey, for example, conducted his eastern campaigns with a number of *legati* in attendance. Under the principate, a man became a *legatus* of a legion after the praetorship, but the term was usually employed of those to whom the emperor delegated *de facto* control of his provinces (*legatus Augusti pro praetore*), where the term 'propraetore' was used by ex-consuls in order visibly to subordinate them to the emperor's proconsular *imperium*.

**Lex**    A law, which has been passed either by one of the assemblies (*comitia*) of the whole people (*populus*), or by the assembly of the plebeians (*concilium, plebis*). Under the principate, the participation of these bodies became a mere formality.

**Libertas**    'Freedom' had a wide collection of meanings in Rome, though that most frequently mentioned was the traditional *freedom* of the nobility to progress along the *cursus honorum* without undue interference from others. It was this *libertas* that was seen as being in conflict particularly with the principle of hereditary succession.

**Maiestas**    Treason. Formally bringing about a charge of treason could be time-consuming. When dealing with conspirators involved in plots it was much more common to hold an *ad hoc* hearing in the senate or even *in camera* to ensure their quick execution, even though their crime was that of treason. This is particularly evident during the reign of Gaius.

**Nobilis**    Literally, one who was 'known'; the *nobiles* (aristocracy) defined themselves as deriving from families which had reached the consulship in earlier generations, and regarded the consulship as virtually their birthright.

**Optimates**    The *optimates* (or self-styled 'best men') during the Republic were those *nobiles* who felt that their factional domin-ance should be exercised primarily through an influential senate taking the leading role in government. It was effectively the *optimates*, with their blinkered view or Rome and its Empire, who forced Caesar and Pompey to war in 49 BC, and who were instru-mental in Caesar's assassination five years later. In the early prin-cipate they and their descendants found the family of the Claudii a more suitable rallying point than that of the Julii.

**Ornamenta praetoria**    The insignia of a *praetor*.

**Pater patriae**    An honorific title, 'father of the country'. It was awarded to Cicero in 63 BC for his defeat of Catiline's conspiracy, and was held by Roman emperors after it had been given to Augustus in 2 BC.

**Patrician**   Traditionally the oldest part of Rome's aristocracy who in the Republic's early days exercised the decisive role in government, maintaining a stranglehold through law and patronage over the political, military, legal and religious machinery of the state. The 'struggle of the orders' (traditionally 509–287 BC) gave more equality to *rich* plebeians, so that the real effectiveness of the distinction between the classes was eroded. Subsequently, the main factional groups (*optimates* and *populares*) each contained members of both classes. Augustus tried to revive the patriciate as the central core of his patronised aristocracy. Patricians were debarred from holding plebeian offices, such as the tribunate of the plebs and the plebeian aedileship.

**Pietas**   The 'sense of duty' to gods, state and family that represented the traditional loyalties of the Roman noble, and which Augustus tried to exemplify and revitalise.

**Pontifex Maximus**   The head of the *pontifices*, the most important priestly college in Rome, which was made up of 16 nobles under Augustus.

**Populares**   The term, meaning 'mob-panderers', was coined by the *optimates* to describe the way in which their opponents appeared to devalue the senate's role in government, and to place their emphasis on manipulating the popular assemblies. The first notable *popularis* was Ti. Sempronius Gracchus (tribune of the plebs in 133 BC). Although the term fell into disuse after the Republic, nobles of this view tended to identify with the Julian family of Augustus, perhaps reflecting Caesar's position of primacy amongst the *populares* in the 50s and 40s BC.

**Praefectus**   Under the principate, the term 'prefect' was applied to various grades within the reformed equestrian order, from the commands of auxiliary army units to some of the highest officers in the order (*praefecti* of Egypt and of the praetorian guard).

**Praetor**   This was the office second in importance to the consulship, although the praetors may in the earliest days have been the chief magistrates – *prae-itor* meaning 'one who goes in front'. From Sulla's time they had an increasing importance as the presiding officers in the courts (*quaestiones*); the post led on to legionary commands and/or governorships of second-rank provinces.

**Princeps**   The term 'chief man' was favoured by Augustus as a form of address; it did not imply a particular office, but throughout the Republic had been applied to those who, in or out of office, were deemed to be prestigious, influential and disposers of patronage.

**Princeps iuventutis**   An honorific title, 'leader of youth'. Sometimes bestowed on young members of the imperial family – such as Gaius and Lucius Caesar, Tiberius Gemellus and Nero.

**Princeps senatus**   A Republican term applied to the man who in terms of seniority (however conceived) was placed at the head of the list of senators, as Augustus was after the *lectio senatus* of 28 BC.

**Proconsul**   The term was originally applied to a consul whose *imperium* had been extended beyond his term of office as consul to enable him to continue command of an army; by the second century BC it was regularly applied to those who commanded provinces after their year of office in Rome: during the principate it was used of the governors (whether ex-consuls or ex-praetors) of senatorial provinces.

**Procurator**   The term was used of various grades of equestrian in the emperor's financial service – from the chief agents in the provinces, down to quite minor officials in their departments. They were officially distinguished by an adjective describing their different salary levels.

**Quaestor**   A financial post and an important step in the *cursus honorum*. It was necessary to hold this position before moving on to become a *praetor*.

**Respublica**   This word, often used emotively to describe the nature of the state which Augustus supplanted after Actium, means simply 'the public concern'. By definition, therefore, it would be negated by anyone with overwhelming and capriciously exercised power (*dominatio*).

**Senatus consultum** The decree issued at the end of a senatorial debate which was not *legally* binding, but an advisory statement passing on the senate's opinion to those popular bodies responsible for making the final decisions and passing laws.

**Tribune of the plebs** Originally appointed, according to tradition, in 494 BC, the tribunes were officers charged with defending their fellow plebeians against injustices perpetrated by patricians. The decisive elements in their 'armoury' were the 'veto', by which they could bring any business (except that of a dictator) to a halt, and the 'sacrosanctity', by which all plebeians were bound by oath to defend an injured or wronged tribune. Gradually, the tribunes were drawn into the regular business of office-holding – almost, but not quite, part of the *cursus honorum*; their veto was employed increasingly as a *factional* weapon, and they became potentially powerful through their ability to legislate with the plebeian assembly without prior consultation with the senate. Under the principate, little of their power remained, dominated as it was by the emperor's tribunician power (*tribunicia potestas*). Augustus, because he was by adoption a patrician, could not hold the office of tribune, though between 36 and 23 BC he acquired most of the powers of the office, and outwardly used them as the basis of his conduct of government in Rome. The power served to stress his patronage and protection of all plebeians.

**Triumvirate** Any group of *three* men; the first triumvirate of 60 BC was the informal arrangement for mutual assistance between Pompey, Crassus and Caesar; the second triumvirate of 43 BC was the legally based 'office' of Octavian, Antony and Lepidus. The term continued to be used of occasional groups of three, and regularly of the three mint officials (*triumviri*, or *tresviri, monetales*) and the punishment officials (*triumviri*, or *tresviri, capitales*), both of which groups were sections of the board of 20, or vigintivirate, the first posts on the senatorial *cursus honorum*.

# APPENDIX 3

# CHRONOLOGY OF MAIN EVENTS

AD

| | |
|---|---|
| 12 | Birth of Gaius |
| 14 | Gaius goes to Gaul and Germany with family |
| | Death of Augustus and accession of Tiberius |
| 17 | Germanicus' triumph in Rome |
| | Gaius and family go to the East |
| 18 | Gaius gives speech in Assos |
| 19 | Death of Germanicus |
| 20 | Gaius returns to Italy with Agrippina |
| 27 | Gaius moves in with Livia |
| 29 | Death of Livia |
| 31 | Death of brother Nero |
| | Gaius moves to Capreae |
| | Death of Sejanus |
| 33 | Gaius made *quaestor* |
| | Deaths of Agrippina and Drusus |
| 35 | Named as heir with Gemellus |
| 36 | Herod Agrippa in Capreae |
| 37 | Death of Tiberius |
| | Accession of Gaius |
| | Remains of Agrippina and Nero recovered |
| | Death of Antonia |
| | Gaius holds his first consulship |
| | Dedication of Temple of Augustus |
| | Gaius suffers an illness |
| 38 | Abolition of sales tax |
| | Restoration of elections to the people |
| | Deaths of Macro and Ennia |
| | Death and consecration of Drusilla |
| | Riots in Alexandria; Flaccus arrested |
| 39 | Gaius holds second consulship |
| | Restoration of *maiestas* trials |
| | Bridge of boats at Baiae |
| | Restructuring of Africa |

Prosecution of Sabinus and his wife
Gaius and army march to the Rhine
Deaths of Lepidus and Gaetulicus
Sisters Agrippina and Livilla banished
Disturbance at Jamnia

40 Gaius holds third consulship
Gaius meets Adminius
Gaius meets Philo and the Jewish deputation
Petronius supposedly ordered to erect the statue at Jerusalem
Ptolemy executed and rebellion in Mauretania

40 Gaius celebrates an ovation

41 Gaius holds fourth consulship
Assassination of Gaius
Accession of Claudius

54 Death of Claudius

# NOTES

## 3 DOMESTIC POLICY

1 See Barrett (1989, 224).
2 See Frank (1940) for a full discussion of the economics surrounding the issue.
3 See Barrett (1996, 57) for an explanation of the Roman tradition on this matter.
4 See Barrett (1989, 194–5).
5 See Millar (1967, 177).
6 See Simpson (1981) for a discussion of this issue.
7 See Brunt (1977).

## 4 FOREIGN POLICY

1 See both Balsdon (1934a, 194) and Barrett (1989, 120).
2 See Barrett (1989, 118).
3 See Garzetti (1974, 98).
4 Gaius' military exploits on the Rhine and Channel have been much debated; for various opinions see the Bibliography, particularly Balsdon (1934a, 1934b), Davies (1966), Bicknell (1968), Garzetti (1974) and Barrett (1989).
5 See Balsdon (1934a, 69).
6 See Bicknell (1968, 501–4).
7 See Campbell (1984, 398–400).
8 See Ferrill (1991, 127–9).
9 For a full discussion of the Jews under Caligula, and the Jewish literary sources, see the works by Smallwood and Bilde in the Bibliography.
10 See Bell (1924).
11 See Smallwood (1961, 10).
12 See Barrett (1989, 187).
13 See Bilde (1978, 85).
14 See Bilde (1978, 88).
15 See Barrett (1989, 224).

## 6 GAIUS AND THE SENATE

1 See Shotter (1992, 27–37) for a discussion of the senate under Tiberius.
2 See Alston (1998, 69).

### 7 CONCLUSION

1 See Momigliano (1934, 1).

## APPENDIX 1: THE SOURCES

1 For a detailed description of the original first-century historians and the possible nature of their works, see Balsdon (1934a, 222–8). See the Bibliography for works on all the major literary sources.

# BIBLIOGRAPHY

Alston, R. (1998) *Aspects of Roman History. AD 14–117*, London: Routledge.

Bagnall, R.S. (1991) 'A Trick a Day to Keep the Tax Man at Bay', *Bulletin of the American Society of Papyrologists* 28, 5–12.

Baldwin, B. (1983) *Suetonius*, Amsterdam: Adolf M Hakkert.

Balsdon, J.P.V.D. (1934a) *The Emperor Gaius*, Oxford: Oxford University Press.

Balsdon, J.P.V.D. (1934b) 'Notes Concerning the Principate of Gaius', *Journal of Roman Studies* 24, 13–24.

Balsdon, J.P.V.D. (1936) 'Gaius and the Grand Cameo of Paris', *Journal of Roman Studies* 26, 152–60.

Barnes, T.D. (1984) 'The Composition of Cassius Dio's Roman History', *Phoenix* 38, 740–55.

Barrett, A.A. (1977) 'Gaius' Policy in the Bosporus', *Transactions of the American Philological Association* 107, 1–9.

Barrett, A.A. (1989) *Caligula: The Corruption of Power*, London: Routledge.

Barrett, A.A. (1990) 'Claudius, Gaius and the Client Kings', *Classical Quarterly* no. 540, 284–6.

Barrett, A.A. (1996) *Agrippina: Sex, Power and Politics in the Early Empire* (New Haven, Conn.: Yale University Press).

Bell, H.I. (1924) *Jews and Christians in Egypt*, Oxford: Oxford University Press).

Benediktson, D.T. (1989) 'Gaius's Madness: Madness or Interictal Temporal Lobe Epilepsy', *Classical World* 82, 370–5.

Benediktson, D.T. (1992) 'Gaius's Phobias and Philias: Fear of Seizure?', *Classical Journal* 87, 159–63.

Bicknell, P. (1962) 'Gaius and the Sea Shells', *Acta Classica* 5, 72–4.

Bicknell, P. (1968) 'The Emperor Gaius' Military Activities in AD 40', *Historia* 17, 496–505.

Bilde, P. (1978) 'The Roman Emperor Gaius (Caligula)'s Attempt to Erect his Statue in the Temple of Jerusalem', *Studia Theologica* 32, 67–93.

Bilde, P. (1988) *Flavius Josephus Between Jerusalem and Rome: His Life, his Works and their Importance* (Journal for the Study of the Pseudepigraphia Supplement, series 2, Sheffield).

Braund, D.C. (1985) *Augustus to Nero: A Sourcebook on Roman History 31 BC–AD 68*, London: Routledge.

Brilliant, R. (1969) 'An Early Imperial Portrait of Gaius', *Acta ad Archaeologiam et Artium Historiam Pertinentia*, vol. 4, 13–17.

Brunt, P.A. (1975) 'Stoicism and the Principate', *Papers of the British School at Rome* 43, 7–35.

Brunt, P.A. (1977) 'Lex de Imperio Vespasiani', *Journal of Roman Studies* 67, 95–116.

Burgers, P. (2001) 'Coinage and State Expenditure: The Reign of Claudius', *Historia* 50, 96–114.

Campbell, J. (1984) *The Emperor and the Roman Army*, Oxford: Oxford University Press.

Carter, J. (ed.) (1987) *Cassius Dio: The Roman History: The Reign of Augustus*, London: Penguin.

Cary, M.M. and Scullard, H.H. (1975) *A History of Rome Down to the Reign of Constantine* (3rd edn), London: Macmillan.

Charlesworth, M.P. (1933) 'The Tradition About Gaius', *Cambridge Historical Journal* 4, 105–9.

Charlesworth, M.P. (1935) 'Some Observations on Ruler Cult, Especially in Rome', *Harvard Theological Review* 28, 5–44.

Clarke, G.W. (1965) 'Seneca the Younger Under Gaius', *Latomus* 24, 62–9.

Crook, J. (1955) *Consilium Principis: Imperial Councils and Councillors from Augustus to Diocletian*, Cambridge: Cambridge University Press.

Davies, R.W. (1966) 'The Abortive Invasion of Britain by Gaius', *Historia* 15, 124–8.

van Deman, E. (1924) 'House Of Gaius', *American Journal of Archaeology* 28, 368–99.

Faur, J.C. (1973) 'Caligula et la Mauretanie: La Fin de Ptolemee', *Klio* 55, 249–71.

Faur, J.C. (1978) 'Un discourse de l'empereur Caligula au Senat', *Klio* 60, 439–47.

Ferrill, A. (1991) *Gaius: Emperor of Rome*, London: Thames & Hudson.

Fishwick, D. (1971) 'The Annexation of Mauretania', *Historia* 20, 467–87.

Fishwick, D. and Shaw, B.D. (1979) 'Ptolemy of Mauretania and the Conspiracy of Gaetulicus', *Historia* 25, 491–4.

Flory, M.B. (1988) 'Pearls for Venus', *Historia* 37, 498–504.

Frank, T. (1940) *An Economic Survey of Ancient Rome.* Vol. 5: *Rome and Italy of the Empire*, Baltimore, Md.: Johns Hopkins University Press.

Garzetti, A. (1974) *From Tiberius to the Antonines: A History of the Roman Empire AD 14–192*, London: Methuen.

Gallivan, P.A. (1979) 'The Fasti for the Reign of Gaius', *Antichton* 13, 66–9.

Goldsworthy, A.K. (1996) *The Roman Army at War 100 BC–AD 200*, Oxford: Clarendon Press.

Goodenough, E.R. (1938) *The Politics of Philo Judaeus: Practice and Theory*, (New Haven, Conn.: Yale University Press).

Goodenough, E.R. (1962) *An Introduction to Philo Judaeus*, Oxford: Blackwell.

Goodman, M. (1996) 'Judaea', *Cambridge Ancient History.* Vol. 10: *Augustan Empire: 43 BC–AD 69*, ed. A.K. Bowman, E. Champlin and A. Lintott (2nd edn), Cambridge: Cambridge University Press, 737–81.

Goodyear, F.R.D. (1984) 'Tiberius and Gaius: Their Influence and Views on Literature', *Aufstieg und Niedergang der Römischen Welt* II 32.1, 603–10.

Goud, T.E. (1996) 'The Sources of Josephus' Antiquitates 19', *Historia* 45, 472–82.

Grant, M. (1975) *The Twelve Caesars*, London: Macmillan.

Humphrey, J.W. and Swan, P.M. (1983) 'Cassius Dio on the Suffect Consuls of AD 39', *Phoenix* 37, 324–7.

Hurley, D.W. (1989) 'Gaius in the Germanicus Tradition', *American Journal of Philology* 110, 316–38.

Hurley, D.W. (1993) *An Historical and Historiographical Commentary on Suetonius' Life of Gaius*, Atlanta, Ga.: Scholars Press.

Jakobson, A. and Cotton, H.M. (1985) 'Gaius's Recusatio Imperii', *Historia* 34, 497–503.

Jones, A.H.M. (1968) *Studies in Roman Government and Law*, Oxford: Blackwell.

Jones, H.S. (1926) 'Claudius and the Jewish Question at Alexandria', *Journal of Roman Studies* 16, 17–35.

Katz, R.S. (1972) 'The Illness of Gaius', *Classical World* 65, 223–5.

Katz, R.S. (1977) 'Gaius's Illness Again', *Classical World* 70, 451.

Levick, B.M. (1967) 'Imperial Control of the Elections Under the Early Principate: Commendatio, Suffragatio, and Nominatio', *Historia* 16, 201–30.

McDermott, W.C. (1972) 'Suetonius, Gaius, 50, 3', *Latomus* 31, 527.

McGinn, T. (1989) 'The Taxation of Roman Prostitution', *Helios* 16, 79–110.

Marañon, G. (1956) *Tiberius: A Study in Resentment*, New York: Duell, Sloan & Pearce.

Marsh, F.B. (1931) *The Reign of Tiberius*, Oxford: Oxford University Press.

Masaro, V. and Montgomery, I. (1978) 'Gaius – Mad, Bad, Ill or All Three?', *Latomus* 37, 894–909.

Masaro, V. and Montgomery, I. (1979) 'Gaius (Caligula) Doth Murder Sleep', *Latomus* 38, 699–700.

Millar, F. (1964) *A Study in Cassius Dio*, Oxford: Clarendon Press.

Millar, F. (1967) *The Roman Empire and its Neighbours*, London: Duckworth.

Millar, F. (1977) *The Emperor in the Roman World*, London: Cornell University Press.

Momigliano, A. (1934) *Claudius: The Emperor and his Achievements*, Oxford: Oxford University Press.

Mommsen, T. (1886) *The Provinces of the Roman Empire*, (vols. 1–2, London: Richard Bentley Publishing.

Morgan, M.G. (1973) 'Gaius's Illness Again', *Classical World* 66, 327–9.

Morgan, M.G. (1977) 'Once Again Gaius's Illness', *Classical World* 70, 452–3.

Newbold, R.F. (1975) 'The Spectacles as an Issue Between Gaius and the Senate', *The Proceedings of the African Classical Associations* 13, 30–5.

Phillips, E.J. (1970) 'The Emperor Gaius' Abortive Invasion of Britain', *Historia* 19, 369–74.

Price, S.F.R. (1996) 'The Place of Religion: Rome in the Early Empire', *Cambridge Ancient History* Vol. 10: *Augustan Empire: 43 BC–AD 69*, ed. A.K. Bowman, E. Champlin and A. Lintott (2nd edn), Cambridge: Cambridge University Press, 812–47.

Ramage, E.S. (1983) 'Denigration of Predecessor Under Claudius, Galba, and Vespasian', *Historia* 32, 201–14.

Rajak, T. (1983) *Josephus: The Historian and his Society*, London: Duckworth.

Rich, J.W. (ed.) (1990) *Cassius Dio: The Augustan Settlement*, Warminster: Aris & Phillips.

Ruger, C. (1996) 'Germany', *Cambridge Ancient History*. Vol. 10: *Augustan Empire 43 BC–AD 69*, ed. A.K. Bowman, E. Champlin and A. Lintolt (2nd edn), Cambridge: Cambridge University Press, 517–34.

Sandmel, S. (1979) *Philo of Alexandria: An Introduction*, Oxford: Oxford University Press.

Scramuzza, V.M. (1940) *The Emperor Claudius*, Cambridge, Mass.: Harvard University Press.

Seager, R.J. (1972) *Tiberius*, London: Methuen.

Shotter, D. (1992) *Tiberius Caesar*, London: Routledge.

Simpson, C.J. (1980) 'The "Conspiracy" of AD 39', *Studies in Latin Literature and Roman History* II (Collection Latomus 168), 201–14.

Simpson, C.J. (1981) 'The Cult of the Emperor Gaius', *Latomus* 90, 489–511.

Smallwood, E.M. (1957) 'The Chronology of Gaius' Attempt to Desecrate the Temple', *Latomus* 16, 3–17.

Smallwood, E.M. (ed.) (1961) *Philonis Alexandrini Legatio ad Gaium*, Leiden: Brill Academic Publishers.

Smallwood, E.M. (1976) *The Jews Under Roman Rule*, Leiden: Brill Academic Publishers.

Stewart, Z. (1953) 'Sejanus, Gaetulicus and Seneca', *American Journal of Philology* 74, 70–85.

Swan, M. (1970) 'Josephus A.J. 19.251–2. Opposition to Gaius and Claudius', *American Journal of Philology* 91, 149–64.

Talbert, R.J.A. (1984) *The Senate of Imperial Rome*, Princeton, N.J.: Princeton University Press.

Taylor, L.-R. (1931) *The Divinity of the Roman Emperor*, Middletown, Conn.: Scholars Press.

Veyne, P. (1990) *Bread and Circuses*, trans. B. Pearce, London: Allen Lane.

Villalba, I. and Varneda, P. (1986) *The Historical Method of Flavius Josephus*, Leiden: Brill Academic Publishers.

Wallace-Hadrill, A. (1983) *Suetonius: The Scholar and his Caesars*, London: Duckworth.

Wardle, D. (1991) 'When Did Gaius Die?', *Acta Classica* 34, 158–65.

Wiedemann, T.E.J. (1996) 'Tiberius to Nero', *Cambridge Ancient History*. Vol. 10: *Augustan Empire 43 BC–AD 69*, ed. A.K. Bowman, E. Champlin and A. Lintott (2nd edn), Cambridge: Cambridge University Press, 198–255.

Williamson, R. (1989) *Jews in the Hellenistic World: Philo*, Cambridge: Cambridge University Press.

Willrich, H. (1903) 'Caligula', *Klio* 3, 85–118, 288–317, 397–470.

Wisemen, T.P. (1991) *Death of an Emperor*, Exeter: University of Exeter Press.

Yavetz, Z. (1969) *Plebs and Princeps*, Oxford: Oxford University Press.

Yavetz, Z. (1996) 'Gaius, Imperial Madness and Modern Historiography', *Klio* 78(1), 105–29.

# INDEX

eBooks – at www.eBookstore.tandf.co.uk

# A library at your fingertips!

eBooks are electronic versions of printed books. You can store them on your PC/laptop or browse them online.

They have advantages for anyone needing rapid access to a wide variety of published, copyright information.

eBooks can help your research by enabling you to bookmark chapters, annotate text and use instant searches to find specific words or phrases. Several eBook files would fit on even a small laptop or PDA.

**NEW:** Save money by eSubscribing: cheap, online access to any eBook for as long as you need it.

## Annual subscription packages

We now offer special low-cost bulk subscriptions to packages of eBooks in certain subject areas. These are available to libraries or to individuals.

For more information please contact webmaster.ebooks@tandf.co.uk

We're continually developing the eBook concept, so keep up to date by visiting the website.

# www.eBookstore.tandf.co.uk